At Whatever Cost

THE STORY OF THE DIEPPE RAID

by R. W. THOMPSON

COWARD-McCANN, Inc.   NEW YORK

FIRST AMERICAN EDITION 1957

© 1956 by R. W. Thompson

Originally published in England
under the title *Dieppe at Dawn*

9781131646435
ISBN

Library of Congress Catalog
Card Number: 56-10500

At Whatever Cost

DAWN OFF DIEPPE, AUGUST 19, 1942

The picture was taken by a member of the crew of a destroyer which covered the landing at Dieppe and assisted in the evacuation of the troops later on the same day. *United Press.*

ACKNOWLEDGEMENTS

I wish to thank the Public Relations Department of the War Office for their ready help in obtaining all necessary permissions for the release of the documents pertaining to the Dieppe Raid.

My grateful thanks are also due to H. A. Cordery, Esq., the Cabinet Archivist, and his assistant, Miss Cooper, for their graciousness in making the documents available, and giving me all possible facilities for their study.

CONTENTS

PART ONE

JUBILEE

PART TWO

VANQUISH

8

PART THREE

AFTERMATH

PROLOGUE

THE Dieppe Raid is perhaps the best known and the least known about of all the important actions of the Second World War. The complete facts were never made known to the public, and the scrappy bits and pieces published at the time created a sense of frustration and unease. Even when all the facts are known it remains a controversial affair.

Sir Winston Churchill has written:[1] 'Military opinion seemed unanimous that until an operation on that scale was undertaken no responsible General would take the responsibility of planning for the main invasion.'

Lt.-General H. D. G. Crerar, in a speech to his Canadian officers immediately after the Normandy landings, credited the Dieppe Raid with paving the way and playing a large and vital part in the success of 'Overlord'.

Be these things as they may, here are the facts.

Undoubtedly the Dieppe Raid is one of the most vivid and dramatic episodes in the story of war. On the face of it it must be ranked as a failure, but its objects were deeper than they appear, and those who should know say otherwise. To me the writing of this story has had a special poignancy, and I have worked with a growing sense of nostalgia for those days, so near to us, so rich in memory, and yet so utterly of a past age, lost and gone forever.

Three years after Dieppe, within a week or two, the affairs of men entered into a new phase with the dropping of atomic bombs on Hiroshima and Nagasaki. Old-fashioned warfare in which men confronted men, albeit at times at some considerable range, was nearing its end, with all its human horrors and brutalities, and with all its grandeur, its heroism, loyalty, chivalry, comradeship and virtue. And in its place was a thing called genocide, calling forth new human values, or denying human values.

So I think of Dieppe along with the Charge of the Light Brigade, and with all the other great deeds in the long story that reaches back far beyond Marathon and the defeat of the Athenians

[1] *Churchill Memoirs.*

9

at Syracuse, and on by way of Pultowa, Valmy, Blenheim and Waterloo. Dieppe is of that *genre*. I doubt whether old Miltiades —and certainly not the great Marlborough—would have felt much out of place at Dieppe. They understood well that kind of thing. This was warfare still recognizable in the age-old terms.

I confess I regret the passing of that long phase of human activity when the art of war was a most potent political weapon. Certainly the existence of civilization as we know it, let alone the existence of mankind, was not threatened.

Honour and Glory are not words to use in the same breath with hydrogen bombs, nor even napalm.

My book is history, very old-fashioned history, and I have done my best to set down the facts clearly, resisting the great temptation to enlarge upon them, or to dramatize beyond my actual knowledge these very stirring deeds of brave and simple men of our own age. I have invented nothing. Even the brief snatches of dialogue quoted are authentic, usually word for word, but always sticking to the simple sense of what is known to have been said. For example, Sergeant Dubuc, being a French-Canadian, may have cried, '*Sauve qui peut!*' the moment after he had killed the German guard. He certainly said something very like that in French or English.

I do not think my book will end the controversy about the Dieppe Raid. Even when all the facts are known it remains something of a mystery, at least to me, or at least there is something mysterious about it. I shall let the Canadians have the last word: it is their due. But Sir Winston Churchill has written:

'Dieppe occupies a place of its own in the long story of war, and the grim casualty figures must not class it as a failure.' [1]

Sir Winston, above all, should know.

[1] *Churchill Memoirs*, Vol. IV.

PART ONE

JUBILEE

CHAPTER ONE

JUBILEE SAILS

ON THE night of August 18th, 1942, two hundred and fifty-two little ships moved out of four English South Coast ports bound on one of the most hazardous adventures of the war. They planned to sail at speed, and in close formations, through the enemy minefields over seventy miles of narrow seas, unseen, unheard, unheralded, and finally to assault by surprise the heavily defended seaport of Dieppe and the immediate flanking beaches. The assault was planned to begin in the Nautical Twilight before the dawn; that is to say, at ten minutes to five o'clock on the morning of August 19th. For the duration of a single tide they were resolved to take the Nazi Führer by the forelock, and at the worst to sow some seeds of fear that might grow to disturb the enemy over all that 'iron held' coast of France.

By nightfall on August 19th the expedition planned to be safely home again in England, in those four ports, Portsmouth, Southampton, Shoreham and Newhaven, from which they sailed.

This is the story of those few hours, thick in the main with disaster, yet shot through with many strands of heroism and steadfastness, and flanked with feats of great daring, that should make this bold and terrible adventure unforgettable in the story of war. It was more than a failure: it helped to pave the way to success.

At 12.15 p.m. on August 18th, the 9th and 13th mine-sweeping flotillas sailed from Portsmouth to open two channels through the enemy minefields to France. They moved by the inshore route towards Newhaven, for if the enemy should observe them on this course their especial purpose would not be suspect.

Meanwhile, under cover of smoke, twenty-four tank landing craft had safely received their burdens of Churchill tanks, and throughout the afternoon and evening of the day a total assault force of 6,086 officers and men was embarked on nine infantry landing ships, and a host of smaller vessels. There was no hitch, nor semblance of a hitch, in all these well-practised preliminaries.

At 6.10 p.m. the mine-sweepers laid the first green flag *Dan* in position to mark the entrance to the westernmost of the two mine-swept channels, and soon afterwards, in the dusk, the Newhaven force sailed. The moon was still high, and the half-light difficult. The leading vessel was almost upon the guiding Dan when a cloud passing over the moon intensified the darkness and gave the look-outs a moment of clear vision. There was no margin of time for casting round. The urgency was to press on. The way was clear ahead.

At ten minutes past nine o'clock the leading infantry landing ship, H.M.S. *Princess Astrid*, cleared the gate of Portsmouth defences, leading the main body of the force. Behind her came the Headquarters ship, the destroyer H.M.S. *Calpe*, followed by the destroyers *Garth*, *Berkeley*, *Albrighton* and *Bleasdale*. These formed at once ahead and altered course to make the western channel. Even then, at that hour, the Dan buoys and the motor launch marking the channel were only sighted two minutes before the *Calpe* reached the channel. She had not reduced speed. Without faltering for a moment she led the way through.

By now the whole expedition was under way, the ships steaming fast in tight formations out of Southampton Water and Shoreham, all converging through these narrow mine-swept channels. Even at this stage the expedition was hazardous. Time was vital even to a minute, and the fine navigation that was essential would not be enough. Luck was also needed, and luck there was. The infantry landing ship, H.M.S. *Queen Emma*, following closely upon the destroyers, and herself leading three groups of landing ships, lost touch with the destroyers, and went through the eastern channel, overtaking the Reserve Headquarters ship, H.M.S. *Fernie*, and a number of small craft. Fine seamanship alone could scarcely have avoided collision, but there was no collision.

Meanwhile the gunboat *Locust*, earmarked for a most daring role in the final adventure, was unable to find the mine-swept channel and went simply through the minefield without hesitation, trusting to luck. There was no time for second thoughts, and *Locust* went through unscathed.

At 9.30 that night the nine infantry landing ships, carrying the main body of the attacking force, shed the disguises that had given them the semblance of merchantmen through all the period of preparation. All depended now on the successful navigation of the mine-swept channels and the avoidance of any clash with the enemy. The moon set that night two hours after midnight. The sea was moderate, the wind freshening from the south–south–west. The two hundred and fifty-two ships, keeping stations in tight groups, were hard on the sterns of the mine-sweeping flotillas in almost total darkness, but for the faint green lights of the guiding Dans. Complete wireless silence was imposed.

The last Dan was laid at two minutes to one o'clock, and ten minutes later the mine-sweepers turned for home. At sixteen minutes past one o'clock the Headquarters ship *Calpe* signalled reduce speed to 18 knots. The convoy was almost through. They would be on time. High tide at Dieppe on that morning would be at three minutes past five.

Capt. J. Hughes-Hallett, R.N., the Naval Force Commander aboard the *Calpe*, was glad to have this first difficulty behind him. It was his job to get the attacking force there on time, to put them ashore, and finally to get them back. He had considered the opening hazards with meticulous care, and had briefed his whole convoy accordingly. He had been resolved, even at this late hour, and in the face of a possible combination of calamities, to call off the whole adventure. He bore a heavy burden of responsibility, and welcomed it. This adventure was his, more perhaps than any other one man's. He had been present at the birth of the idea. He had lived with it all through, and only at the last moment, to his great pride and joy, had he been given command of the Naval Force.

As it was, the voyage had been almost without incident. At half past eleven a hand grenade had exploded in the infantry landing ship, H.M.S. *Invicta*, wounding seventeen men of the South Saskatchewan Regiment. That was all.

At five minutes to three o'clock the infantry landing ships began to put their assault craft into the water, while their naval escorts manœuvred to stations ready to lead them in. The whole armada of little ships was safely assembled, its presence unsuspected, and within easy reach of the enemy-held coast. There were no sounds of aircraft overhead. The radar screens were clear. The wireless silence remained unbroken. The timings were exactly according to plan. This was the point of no return.

CHAPTER TWO

THE BIRTH OF THE PLAN

I

THE idea of an attack on Dieppe was first considered by the Target Committee of Combined Operations Headquarters under Capt. J. Hughes-Hallett, R.N., early in April 1942. The Germans had been building up the coastal defences of France ever since their defeat in the Battle of Britain in the Winter of 1940. Many French ports still held the Nazi invasion barges, but as the Nazi hopes of invading Britain had dwindled, their fears had increased. The constant talk of a second front urged them to ever greater efforts to make the Channel coast impregnable.

The day must come when we should have to invade France, and it was here across the Channel, somewhere on this Northern coast of France, that it would have to be. It seemed vital at an early date to test the German defences. Somehow experience must be gained, and at whatever cost.

From the outset the main intention inspiring the idea of a raid as ambitious as that on Dieppe was to gain experience for the future, and inevitable, large-scale operations. And, above all, that intention remained the real object of the Dieppe Raid, and was the ruling factor in the plan that was made.

Dieppe seemed a natural objective for testing purposes, and since the Summer of 1940 it had held an average of forty invasion barges. As a side issue it appealed to naval minds to steal these craft. Dieppe is a good port. It was known to be well defended, and its seaway well covered by heavy batteries, particularly to the east of Dieppe, near Berneval, and to the west behind Varengeville-sur-Mer and Quiberville. These batteries, known respectively as the Goebbels battery and the Hess battery, would make it impossible to keep a naval force off Dieppe. From Berneval to Quiberville is a distance of approximately eleven miles, with Dieppe itself approximately two miles east of centre.

The Goebbels and Hess batteries would have to be silenced, for the scale of the raid envisaged would make it necessary to hold a considerable number of ships off Dieppe for a period up to twelve hours, through all the operation of landing and withdrawal. These two batteries were therefore the natural outer flanks of any attack on Dieppe from the sea.

On the 14th April representatives of the General Staff, Home Forces, joined the Planning syndicate and got down to work on a hard plan to raid Dieppe in force. Lt.-General B. L. Montgomery, C.B., D.S.O., then G.O.C.-in-C. South-Eastern Command, was closely associated with the military side of the planning, and as soon as it was decided to use Canadian troops for the main body of the raiding force, the Canadian, Lt.-General H. D. G. Crerar, G.O.C. 1st Canadian Corps, was brought in.

A study of Dieppe and its flanking beaches of Puits and Pourville, within the outer flanking limits of the batteries at Berneval and Varengeville–Quiberville, gives the outline of the task to be filled in. It is a coastline of vertical chalk cliffs from thirty to one hundred feet high, and broken by river valleys and narrow steep-sided gulleys. A flat drying rocky ledge extends seaward for an average of half a mile from the face of the cliffs. It is of slippery wave-cut chalk. All the beaches are of shingle with flint stones from 3–6 inches in diameter, and with sand at low tide.

On all that stretch of coast, backed by downland two or three hundred feet above sea level, and almost treeless except in the regions of the small coastal villages, the most conspicuous landmark, apart from Dieppe itself, is the octagonal tower of the Pointe d'Ailly lighthouse, which stands above the rounded summit of the point separating Varengeville from Quiberville, and almost at the extreme western flank of the proposed attack. It was camouflaged green and yellow, but its silhouette sticks up above the skyline, and is almost always clearly visible from the sea.

Dieppe itself lies in a mile-wide gap at the mouth of the River D'Arques. Its beaches, backed by two wide boulevards, lawns and gardens and a line of hotels, extend for about 1,500 yards from the western leg of the harbour jetty, and are flanked by two headlands. It is at once obvious that these headlands are formidable obstacles. They dominate the whole area of beach. An effort must therefore be made to outflank these headlands from the neighbouring beaches of Puits to the east and Pourville to the west. Indeed, if the object is simply to raid Dieppe, to hold it for a few hours, destroy plant, gain enemy information, blow up the port and remove forty-odd invasion barges, it is unlikely that any planner would have considered a frontal assault on the Dieppe beaches, save perhaps as a feint or diversion. As it was, there was much discussion on this point when the first formal meeting of the Planning Committee took place on 25th April, under the chairmanship of the Chief of Combined Operations, Vice-Admiral Lord Mountbatten.

The frontal assault, together with powerful flanking attacks, was finally adopted. Bearing in mind the real object of the raid the decision may be justified. It is either an operation to gain vital information for the final blueprint for invasion, or it is simply a raid on a very large scale, and with limited harassing objectives. Men and probably tanks had to be landed in force in face of the enemy. Air and naval support had to be provided. It had to be a rehearsal for invasion, and in a limited way it had to look like invasion.

I do not pretend to a special knowledge of the many discussions and arguments relevant to this raid that took place in the early stages, but the Planners must have been acutely aware that the raid would carry with it great dangers of being misunderstood by everyone; by the French people, by the British people, by the Allies, and perhaps especially by the Canadians, whose troops would bear the brunt for good or ill. Perhaps it mattered least of all what the Germans might think. But it was almost certain that unless the raid was an outward and visible success as a raid those responsible would be as much harassed by their own side as by the enemy. They were prepared for this to happen. They would have to sit quiet and say nothing, or very little.

There was little time for speculations of this nature: perhaps not enough. The need was for hurry. The number of days in each month of high Summer on which the operation could take place are put by some authorities as low as two. Certainly they are very limited, and could be eliminated completely by adverse weather. The German Command had their troops and defences in the area in the highest state of readiness for the periods from the end of June to 21st July, and from the 1st to the 19th August. The 19th August was the outside possible date on which the raid could take place in that year of 1942. Even the tide variations from one week to the next could upset the carefully worked out timings of all the detail of action.

Under the code name RUTTER the operation went ahead fast. The main force for the attack on the beaches of Dieppe and its immediate flanks was selected from the 4th and 6th Canadian Infantry Brigades of the 2nd Canadian Division, a final total of 298 officers and 4,663 other ranks of the Canadian Army. This force[1] went into special training early in May at Bridport, while the naval craft were earmarked and assembled in their ports. Inevitably there would be changes, but it was vital that as many officers and men as possible should study and practise their roles.

The exact method of attacking the flanking batteries and the strength of the air support to be used had not yet been decided.

In May and June, while the troops took part in two major exercises named YUKON 1 and 2, the detail of the plan took shape. There were to be five main points of attack:

East of Dieppe:
  (i) BERNEVAL
  (ii) PUITS
  (iii) DIEPPE
West of Dieppe:
  (iv) POURVILLE
  (v) VARENGEVILLE–QUIBERVILLE

The method was swiftly developed and filled in. The discussion now centred on the question of tactical surprise. At that time the best military minds in the West thought surprise essential. It is, I believe, the heart of the matter: should such an attack —should, in fact, invasion of the enemy coast—be preceded by bombardment, or not?

Strategic surprise was, of course, impossible. Even tactical surprise posed great problems, and must be subject to luck in great degree. The whole force must be moved across the Channel unknown to the enemy, and its presence and intention must not be discovered until the attacks go in.

The decision was made to attempt tactical surprise. It is a measure of the importance attached to it at that date.

The limitations of tide, time and weather were factors of the utmost consequence. It had been decided to use paratroops, or glider-borne troops, for the outer flank attacks on the batteries,

[1] Appendix 9. Order of Battle.

Goebbels and Hess, and this decision increased the importance of the weather. Finally there was the problem of the length of time it might be possible to maintain the force off Dieppe in full view of the enemy, and how much time would be necessary to achieve results. It was a question of two tides or one. Even confining the operation to a single tide would mean that a large number of ships would have to maintain themselves and perform their vital roles of assistance to the troops for a period of at least 9 to 10 hours from the moment of revelation or first assault to the final withdrawal. All this time they would be in easy sight and close range of the enemy artillery, and the focus of all the air power—and possibly naval power—he could bring to bear. Our own air cover would have to be very great, and the difficulties of maintaining it in the necessary strength would become very heavy indeed as time went by.

The final decision was to confine the operation to one tide.

From the outset it was apparent that the timings would be vital, and that there could be almost no latitude at all. Fifteen minutes late at any of the five main points of attack could mean disaster, not only in the local area, but to the entire operation. A jig-saw must be constructed in which every piece must fit, and in which little or nothing was left to chance.

Meanwhile the second exercise YUKON had gone off much better than the first, and the prospects for Operation RUTTER looked promising. A date was fixed for the raid in early July.

Intelligence had provided very full reports, including the detailed maps of defences. Scale models were built covering the whole area of the proposed raid, and all discernible batteries, beach defences, machine-gun posts, anti-tank blocks and radar stations marked. This model was photographed from a very low angle from seaward to represent the coast at Nautical Twilight. There were 770 copies made of these silhouettes with all the landing places marked in the representative colours chosen for them, and these were issued to Flotilla leaders and all officers commanding ships.

All possible information in regard to the beaches, defences, and enemy strength was meticulously gathered, constantly added to, correlated and assessed. Air reconnaissance sorties were constantly flown to obtain further photographic information. The Churchill tanks for the operation were fully tested over the kind of shingle and on the gradients they would encounter, and they were also water-proofed to a depth of six feet.

Early in July the raid was ready to sail. The troops were embarked. And then at the last moment a hit-or-miss air attack put two of the infantry landing ships out of action. These were H.M.S. *Princess Astrid* and H.M.S. *Josephine Charlotte*. The raid was cancelled, and the troops disembarked, many of them in some mental confusion, not knowing whether this had been the real thing or simply another exercise.

2

There followed a period of forty-one days when it was almost impossible to prevent speculative talk. The security people had a difficult and anxious time. The troops went back into training. The Planning Committee further revised their plans. They made one important change. The limiting factors of time, tide and weather gave so narrow a margin that the whole project was in danger. The use of airborne troops for the outer flank attacks on the batteries was therefore abandoned, and their role given to Special Service Commandos. Operation RUTTER was dead. Operation JUBILEE was born in its stead.

On the morning of the 17th August the Chief of Combined Operations in consultation with the Force Commanders and the C.-in-C. Portsmouth decided to go ahead. It was the last possible moment. The raid would be sailed on the night of 18th/19th August. At ten o'clock on the morning of 17th August the preliminary order was issued.

A last photo reconnaissance was flown. It flew very low over the harbour entrance to Dieppe, and the photographs revealed the suspected presence of pill-boxes concealed in the caves of the Eastern headland. It also revealed a tank encased in a concrete wall at the end of the Western breakwater.

In the early afternoon of 17th August the Chief of Combined Operations received the following weather forecast:

'Winds will be South Westerly, light, and remain so for whole period. . . . Risk that wind will increase to moderate late in afternoon. Weather fair during day, fine during night.

Visibility 8–15 miles with local haze by day, decreasing 2–5 miles. Sea smooth. No swell.'

Later in the day this weather forecast was revised:

'Winds will increase from S.S.W. early in forecast period becoming moderate to fresh, and veering to W.S.W. early to-morrow. . . . Rain and poor visibility will spread across the area during the night. Sea smooth, becoming moderate. Swell slight.'

Nothing better could be hoped for. It was the last chance. A final conference held at Tangmere discussed the use of heavy bombers, and decided against. A total of sixty-seven squadrons mainly of fighter aircraft were to be committed. In the mind of Air Marshal Leigh-Mallory, commanding this side of the operation from his headquarters, No 11 Group Fighter Command, there was no doubt that this would be a major challenge to the German Air Force. He hoped they would accept it. It could be the biggest thing since the Battle of Britain.

Vice-Admiral Lord Mountbatten, together with Lt.-General H. D. G. Crerar, joined Air Marshal Leigh-Mallory at No. 11 Group Headquarters. The detailed maps of the whole operation were before them. They would be in radio contact with the Force Commanders on board the Headquarters ship *Calpe* from the first moment of assault.

Major-General H. F. Roberts commanded the Military Force. Air Commodore Cole was Air Liaison Officer afloat. Capt. J. Hughes-Hallett commanded the Naval Force.[1] Every man knew his part.

3

The Naval Force sailed that night of 18th August organized in thirteen groups, the whole force escorted by eight destroyers. These destroyers, supported by Steam Gun Boats (S.G.B.'s), Motor Gun Boats (M.G.B.'s) and Motor Launches (M.L.'s), represented the heaviest fire-power the Naval Force could bring to bear in its own defence and in support of the landings.

[1] Appendix 8. Chain of Command. Order of Battle.

The nine Infantry Landing Ships (L.S.I.'s) carrying the main body of the Military Force, were in Groups 1, 2, 3 and 4, closely escorted by flotillas of motor and steam gun boats. These infantry landing ships, H.M.S. *Princess Astrid, Princess Beatrix, Invicta, Glengyle, Duke of Wellington, Prince Charles, Leopold, Queen Emma* and *Prince Albert*, had to be shepherded, with immense care, through the minefield. The loss of the *Princess Astrid* alone would have meant the abandonment of the operation.[1]

Groups 5, 6 and 7 consisted of 74 Large Personnel Landing Craft (L.C.P.'s (L)) escorted by steam gun boats, one motor launch and one Large Landing Craft Flak (L.C.F. (L)).

In Groups 8, 9, 10, 11 and 12 were the 24 Tank Landing Craft (L.C.T.'s) escorted by motor launches and flak landing craft.

Group 13 comprised the 7 Fighting French Chasseurs, escorted by the sloop H.M.S. *Alresford*.

Together with the Headquarters ship, the destroyer H.M.S. *Calpe*, and the reserve Headquarters ship, the destroyer H.M.S. *Fernie*, a total of 252 ships of all shapes, sizes and varying speeds made up the force that had assembled and finally sailed in the wake of the 9th and 13th Mine-sweeping Flotillas in almost total darkness.

On board these ships Major-General H. F. Roberts had under his direct command, 298 Officers and 4,663 Other Ranks of the Canadian Army, 65 Officers and 992 Other Ranks of Nos. 3, 4 and 6 Commandos, and the Royal Marine Commando, 18 Officers and Men of the Inter-Allied Commando, and 50 Officers and Men of the 1st Ranger Battalion, U.S. Army.

In the air, in close support of the raid in attack and to provide air cover throughout, there would be 60 squadrons of fighter aircraft, including 4 squadrons of Army Co-operation Tactical Reconnaissance Mustangs, and there would be 7 squadrons of bombers and fighter-bombers. Already throughout the hours of darkness Coastal Command were flying patrols of Anti-Surface Vessel aircraft in the Channel.[2]

The Plan confronting Major-General Roberts in his Operations Room on board H.M.S. *Calpe* was of the utmost simplicity in its broad outline. The whole scope of the attack and the Order of

[1] Order of Naval Force Commander. Appendix 1.
[2] See Appendix 2.

Battle of his troops could be taken in at a glance on his maps. From Left to Right the beaches had been allotted colours. The five main points of attack had developed eight final heads. The four flank attacks would go in in the Nautical Twilight, followed thirty minutes later by a main assault on Dieppe itself.[1]

Left Flank:
  East of Dieppe
            Beach opposite *Berneval*   — YELLOW 1
            Beach at *Belleville-sur-Mer*   — YELLOW 2
  Inner Left Flank:
            Beach at *Puits*   — BLUE
Centre:
  Dieppe
Centre Left: East Beach   — RED
Centre Right: West Beach   — WHITE
  West of Dieppe
Inner Right Flank:
            Beach at *Pourville*   — GREEN
Right Flank: Beach opposite *Varengeville*   — ORANGE 1
            Beach ¼ mile *East of River Saane*   — ORANGE 2

The Intention of the Raid is expressed briefly as follows:

   (*a*) Destroying enemy defences in vicinity of Dieppe.
   (*b*) Destroying aerodrome installations at St. Aubyn.
   (*c*) Destroying R.D.F. stations, power stations, dock and rail facilities, and petrol dumps in vicinity.
   (*d*) Removing invasion barges for own use.
   (*e*) Removal of secret documents from Divisional Headquarters at Arques la Bataille.
   (*f*) Capture prisoners.

Few could know better than the Military Force and Naval Force Commanders as the infantry landing ships began to put their assault craft into the water slightly ahead of time that minutes were more vital to the success of this dangerous enterprise even than human heroism and resource.

[1] See Appendix 3.

THREE O'CLOCK IN THE MORNING

I

As soon as they emerged from the minefield on that early morning of 19th August the two hundred and fifty-two little ships began at once to move to their positions for the attack. The sounds they made, the murmur and rustle of the waters against them, the stir of screws, and the precise yet muffled staccato of subdued voices, were little more than undertones beneath the natural sounds of wind and water. They had come safely through the main obstacles of the night, and now the enemy citadel lay before them, invisible in the darkness. There was an extraordinary quality of suspense, as there is when a body of men crawl under cover of darkness over open ground towards their target, a sense of stealth in which the least untoward sound rings out like the harsh clang of a cracked gong.

At once the destroyers began to fan out in wide arcs to east and west on their protective flanking duties, while the central pattern at the heart of the convoy began to stir into its varied shapes, as though in the performance of some grave ritual dance. Through all the night the wireless silence had remained unbroken. Unseen, almost unheard even by its nearest neighbour, each ship felt itself an integral part of this assorted pack, held together by something that seemed akin to that telepathic sense that weaves flights of birds into coherent movement. Once through the minefield, this sense had heightened as the ships emerged into a new element of danger and began to engage themselves in that sombre ordered pattern that must precede the final crisis.

At three o'clock in the morning the infantry landing ships carrying the men who would assault the Blue and Green Beaches of the inner flanks at Puits and Pourville were due to lower their landing craft. Their assault landings had to be synchronized with those of the commandos on the outer flanks, exactly half an hour after the beginning of Nautical Twilight. Visibility would be about two hundred yards. On these timings would hang the success or failure of all the operation. They were ahead of time. At five minutes to the hour H.M.S. *Princess Beatrix* and H.M.S. *Invicta* put their landing craft into the water with the men destined for the Green Beach at Pourville. Three minutes later, and two minutes ahead of time, H.M.S. *Princess Astrid* and H.M.S. *Queen Emma* had the first of their landing craft in the water for the assault on the Blue Beach at Puits. It augured well.

The whole armada had by now taken on the outlines of its five assaults. The left flanking Group 5 led by the Steam Gun Boat 5, with Motor Launch 346 and one flak landing craft, moved steadily out on the eastern flank followed by twenty personnel landing craft carrying No 3 Commando towards the Yellow Beaches of Berneval. The destroyers *Brocklesby* and *Slazak* screened them from sea attack eastward.

Group 1 on the right had lost no time in forming up. The men of No. 4 Commando had been carried in H.M.S. *Prince Albert*, and now in their landing craft they took stations behind Motor Gun Boat 312, and Steam Gun Boat 9, while the destroyers *Bleasdale*, *Albrighton*, *Berkeley* and *Garth* steamed fanwise to screen the whole western flank.

The flotillas of gun boats and motor launches, not allotted at this stage with special roles of leadership of the assault craft, moved swiftly to protective positions. Without fuss, guided only by the precision of the orders, the whole convoy took shape in the darkness in its five main parts. In the centre the destroyers *Calpe* and *Fernie* leading Group 8, had become the focal points of the silent herd of ships that would form the core of the main assault.

Behind Group 8 the sloop *Alresford* led the rearguard group of thirteen Fighting French Chasseurs, with the Motor Launch 344 and one flak landing craft leading the tank landing craft in Group 12.

By half past three the whole pattern was almost worked out as quietly as on an exercise. But although the pattern was almost faultless in its outward semblance there were small flaws. The flotilla of landing craft carrying the Royal Regiment of Canada discovered themselves formed up behind the wrong gun boat. The two or three minutes they had gained at the outset were lost, and others ticked away while commanders wrestled with the problem in the baffling darkness, and the imposed silence. The infantry landing ships carrying the Royal Regiment had been escorted from Portsmouth by Steam Gun Boat 8 and Motor Gun Boat 316. Now at this crucial moment they had lost contact with the motor gun boat, without which they were a body without a head, and useless. At ten minutes to five o'clock in that swiftly dissolving period of Nautical Twilight, they must land ᴄn the Blue Beach of Puits. Only then could they hope to achieve that measure of surprise that might give them a foothold. Even with time on their side it would not be a simple matter to pick up the meagre landmarks that would lead them into Puits, and none knew this better than the Commander of Motor Gun Boat 316, as he groped in the darkness for the head of his column. Nearly thirty minutes had passed before he found it.

The silence was broken throughout this long-drawn-out half-hour by the subdued but harsh music of leather and steel, by muffled curses and bodies tense in close company, and once by an ominous splash as a company of the Royal Regiment lost its Bangalore torpedoes overboard.

Meanwhile the whole right flank of the expedition had got under way on time towards its tasks. The South Saskatchewan Regiment, carried in H.M.S. *Princess Beatrix* and H.M.S. *Invicta*, were soon into their assault craft led by Lt.-Commander R. M. Prior, D.S.C., R.N., in Motor Gun Boat 317 towards the Green Beach at Pourville. Behind them 25 personnel landing craft of the 2nd, 6th and 7th flotillas, that had brought the Queen's Own Cameron Highlanders from Newhaven, formed up to follow them in at an interval of thirty minutes.

It was essential that the flanking columns should clear the convoy to give space for the central group of the main attack to manœuvre freely. At twenty minutes past three o'clock, precisely on time, H.M.S. *Glengyle*, *Prince Charles* and *Leopold* lowered their landing craft with the men of the frontal assault, and these now, as the flanking groups cleared the body of the convoy, sought their positions behind their gun boats and motor launches. Now again precious minutes were lost as a motor launch strove to make contact in the darkness with the assault craft of *Prince Charles* and *Leopold*. Because of this it took the two flotillas for the main assault on the Dieppe beaches half an hour to form up carrying the Royal Hamilton Light Infantry and the Essex Scottish Regiment.

Lt.-Commander Mullen, R.N., ready to lead in the main assault on Motor Gun Boat 326, was not greatly disturbed. His course lay dead ahead. All he had to do was to go straight in with the dawn light at twenty minutes past five. He thought he would make it on time. The first wave of tank landing craft were already forming up to follow his wake.

Nevertheless, within forty-five minutes of emerging from the minefield, nearly five thousand men had been put safely into landing craft in complete darkness from darkened ships, themselves manœuvring into positions like pieces in a puzzle. Only the flotilla of the inner left flank, like a shortened leg from the parent body, and carrying the Royal Regiment towards Puits, marred the symmetry of the pattern growing on the radar screens of the Headquarters ships *Calpe* and *Fernie*. Measured in terms of time this lame leg was nearly twenty minutes short. It increased the tension in those who watched and waited, knowing well the difficulties of navigation that faced Lt.-Commander H. W. Goulding, D.S.O., R.N., who was leading them in. Puits would be difficult to identify at the best of times, and it seemed even at this hour that it might be the key to the success of the whole main attack.

Lt.-Commander Goulding set his course to sight Dieppe. He would then alter course eastward to pick up the narrow valley of Puits. He was fighting a battle with minutes, picking them up one by one, but there was too little time.

The seas, at any rate, seemed clear of enemy. The wireless silence had remained unbroken. It would only be broken if:

(i) Enemy forces were aware of the presence of our ships.

(ii) By L.S.I. if it appeared likely that the touchdown would be more than fifteen minutes late.

(iii) By the Senior Officer of Group 5 if by delays or casualties the success of the landing at Yellow Beaches was seriously jeopardized.

There were times when the continuing silence, drawing out its minutes, seemed to possess the unbearable tension of a sustained scream. It was infused with a quality of unreality; that all this sea and sky could be at the enemy's gates; that within the hour the dawn would reveal the coast of France. It seemed almost that all this was sheer illusion; that the dawn would reveal nothing— nothing but the sea.

Almost at the precise moment that Lt.-Commander Mullen got under way with the columns for the main assault formed up behind him, flashes of gunfire burst suddenly away to the eastward, tearing jagged rents in the body of the darkness. It was exactly thirteen minutes to four o'clock, a full hour before the fading of Nautical Twilight that meant zero on the flanks. The radar screens were too full of craft, and at the spearheads of the moving columns nothing ominous was visible.

The wireless silence remained unbroken.

2

Less than a minute before it happened there was no hint of danger to the steam gun boat at the head of Group 5 leading in No. 3 Commando at a steady $9\frac{1}{2}$ knots towards the Yellow Beaches of Berneval and Belleville-sur-Mer. With a full hour to go before zero Commander D. B. Wyburd, R.N., staring into the almost opaque darkness from the bridge of the gun boat estimated that the beaches lay no more than eight miles ahead. He was well on time and sure of his ultimate landmarks. The sea was slight, with the wind freshening from the west. The conditions were as good as anyone had dared to hope.

But the silence coupled with the intense darkness was oppressive. Not for a moment throughout this vital stage before the assault had the Commander relaxed his personal vigil on the bridge. His was the responsibility. The shadowy loom of the landing craft immediately astern alone set limits to the enveloping darkness. But the Commander's eyes were fixed ahead, and for all he could possibly know in this drawn-out silence of the long night the steam gun boat might be alone. It gave him comfort that the destroyers *Brocklesby* and *Slazak* must be steaming on zig-zag paths guarding his open flank, alert to intercept an enemy and to protect his precious convoy. There was much on his mind. He knew very well that the destruction of the Goebbels battery behind Berneval was essential to the safety of the naval force that must lie out in the open sea off Dieppe, a sitting target, for many hours. It was a true naval task. He had tried to imagine every possible contingency that might occur on the run in. As he saw it there would not be time to do anything but press on in the event of trouble. Any other course might disorganize the landing craft following on this tenuous thread of vision, and all might lose contact. Whatever happened he was resolved to fight his way through, and had already issued his orders accordingly.

At one moment as the Commander stared into the darkness there was nothing, and then a shadow, a dark shape, unmistakably a ship, loomed on his port bow. Almost on the instant a star shell climbed into the sky to reveal five ships in an arc from port to starboard across his bows. The gun boat's forward guns were blazing as the concentrated fire of heavy A/A and 3–4-inch shells raked her fore and aft, wrecking the wireless gear in the first blast even before a warning signal might have been given.

Commander Wyburd rode the bridge, erect in the face of withering fire at point-blank range, as though to lift his craft by main force through the enemy guns. The gun boat continued to steam dead ahead at 9½ knots. The time as the star shell lit the sky was exactly thirteen minutes to four o'clock. By four o'clock the gun boat was no more than a hulk, her guns silenced, her boilers hit five times, half her crew wounded and bleeding on her decks. Seven minutes later, in the words of the official record, 'S.G.B. 5 was a shambles', barely capable of steaming at 6 knots, and defenceless. The plan to fight a way through had failed.

So swift and intense had been this brief and devastating encounter that it had been impossible to observe the extent of it beyond the bounds of the battered gun boat. It had seemed to Wyburd that each minute must bring the protecting destroyers rushing to his aid, and even at this late hour their arrival could have saved the day. But of the *Brocklesby* and *Slazak* there was no sign.

Meanwhile the flak landing craft, commanded by Lt. A. D. Fear, R.N., had come furiously into the fight, engaging the enemy with her two twin 4-inch guns with such accuracy that she had two of the enemy ships in trouble before they could turn their guns upon her. The enemy convoy had seen the steam gun boat heading straight into their midst out of the night, and had concentrated their whole fire power upon her. The flak landing craft coming in suddenly on their flanks took them by surprise. One enemy vessel was in flames and another sinking before the fire control of Lt. Fear's craft was put out of action; but she had levelled up the score.

There had not been much time or chance for speculation, but now the flames revealed the enemy as a small group of armed trawlers almost certainly bound westward for Dieppe, and now seeking the shelter of the coast and the cover of the remaining darkness. It had been a chance encounter. Two or three minutes either way, and these two groups of ships might have passed each other by unseen. The realization was added gall to Commander Wyburd and Lt.-Colonel Durnford-Slater, in command of No. 3 Commando, on board the disabled gun boat. They were entirely without means of communication. Of their convoy five landing craft had closed with the gun boat, and of the remainder there was no sign. It seemed certain that the Group had scattered, and it was impossible to go ahead with this small rump. On the very threshold of the beaches their high hopes had been dashed by pure chance.

It seemed obvious to the two commanders aboard the wallowing gun boat that Group 5 had ceased to exist as a fighting force, and the Yellow beach landings were impossible. They had good reason to feel dismay, but no time to give way to it. This dire misfortune, they well knew, might jeopardize the success of the whole raid, and they knew, too, that the die was cast as the minutes ticked by. The destroyers *Brocklesby* and *Slazak* might have disappeared from the face of the waters, and this above all was baffling. Motor Launch 346 might be striving to round up stragglers.

But the two commanders had to act on the facts as they knew them, and they had to act quickly. It was certain that the action must have been observed by the *Calpe*, and by every ship in the entire convoy. It might well have alerted the enemy along all that line of coast, and destroyed all hopes of tactical surprise. The wireless equipment was beyond repair.

Grimly Wyburd and Durnford-Slater considered their course. Half the crew of the gun boat were wounded, many of them gravely, and in need of attention. Even the landing craft had not escaped unscathed. Swiftly the commando men aboard one of these were transferred to the gun boat. The other four landing craft were ordered to stand by in readiness to tow the gun boat back to England.

It was five minutes to five o'clock, five minutes after zero and the carefully planned moment of assault on the beaches of Berneval and Belleville, when Commander Wyburd and Lt.-Colonel

Durnford-Slater went aboard the cleared landing craft and set off on their grim mission to find the Headquarters ship *Calpe*, and report the disaster.

At that moment three officers and seventeen men of No. 6 Troop, No. 3 Commando, were ashore on the deserted beach of Belleville, Yellow Beach 2. They had got ashore unseen. Their resolve was clear and simple: to attack the Goebbels battery of four 5.9-inch guns with its garrison of at least 200 men behind Berneval. They had gone in exactly on time.

3

Under the sudden shock and impact of the heavy fire from the five enemy armed trawlers Group 5 had scattered to save itself. In close formation behind the steam gun boat the landing craft were sitting targets for the high explosive sweeping the gun boat's decks. Four were at once badly hit, their crews sustaining killed and wounded, so that only by great determination might they hope even to limp back home across the Channel. Four others, crippled with engine trouble, had fallen far astern and had not reached the scene of the battle. All these eight landing craft finally reached home.

Of the remainder, five had closed the gun boat, resolved to keep with her at all costs, as the surest way to get through. Three others had closed the flak landing craft, and five more had finally come together under the leadership of the motor launch. There were two others. Each of these, finding themselves entirely alone and unsupported, nevertheless held their courses without hesitation for the coast of France.

Through all this time the destroyers *Brocklesby* and *Slazak* continued to steam at a distance of approximately four miles to the N.N.E., judging the fire to be coming from the shore and not to concern them. Not for a moment did it occur to either of them to investigate.

It had seemed at first to those who watched and waited on board the Headquarters ship *Calpe* that the destroyers *Brocklesby* and *Slazak* might have mistaken Group 5 for the enemy. But this thought was swiftly dismissed. As the minutes went by without news, and the firing at last died down, Capt. Hughes-Hallett felt convinced that the destroyers had played their part—if part there had been to play. Theirs was the primary protective role.

The last of the night was running out fast. All along the line the landing craft were closing the beaches in the last minutes before the dawn twilight faded. The burning question was whether the great effort to achieve Tactical surprise had failed in the light of the unexplained battle on the left.

It was fifteen minutes to seven o'clock in the full light of day, and with all that line of coast shrouded in the smoke and din of battle, when Commander Wyburd and Lt.-Colonel Durnford-Slater at last reached the *Calpe* with news of their disaster. They had groped their way for nearly two hours, frustrated at every turn in their grim journey, boarding four ships in vain efforts to get a signal through, until now, as they faced the Force Commanders, their news added only to the fog of war. Very little was clear to the Force Commanders at that hour, but it was certain that whatever disaster had befallen the eastern flank the Goebbels battery behind Berneval had not fired an effective shot, and had scarcely fired at all.

But this was no moment to question miracles. With orders to find his scattered convoy and round up as many landing craft as possible Commander Wyburd set out again for the Yellow Beaches on board the Motor Gun Boat 317. No man could have fought his ship more gallantly than he had done in that fierce encounter of the morning, but even had he been aware of it the knowledge would have brought him little comfort in that hour.

CHAPTER FOUR

THE YELLOW BEACHES

I

ALMOST imperceptibly the darkness was diminishing, and the long night was nearly done. It had seemed at times to Lt. N. T. Buckee, R.N.V.R., in command of his landing craft, that it would go on for ever. It had been a long blind crawl, with the very sea itself almost invisible, until the crash of gunfire had brought an abrupt end to it. At that moment Buckee's blood had quickened, giving him a heightened alertness and keying his senses and his instincts to the business of war. His landing craft, carrying the Commanding Officer and Headquarters Party of No. 6 Troop, 3 Commando, had been holding station to starboard of Group 5. The landing craft with two others was bound for Yellow Beach 2, and Buckee's mind did not consciously reach a decision as he reacted instantly to the moment of crisis. The light of the enemy star shell had given him an indelible vision of the dark pattern of ships. The way was clear ahead, and as the first burst of gunfire crashed over the decks of the gun boat Lt. Buckee was already out of the line of fire holding his course for Belleville-sur-Mer. There he had a rendezvous in the dawn twilight, and he would keep it.

When Buckee did have time to give this instinctive and natural decision a moment of thought it seemed also the surest way of staying with, or meeting, those who shared his mission. He was not given to worrying, and neither was his second-in-command, Sub.-Lt. D. J. Lewis, R.N.V.R.

For more than twenty minutes the naval action blazed astern and in the seeming silence of its end Buckee saw dead ahead the dark unmistakable loom of France like a low wall beneath the sky.

"There it is," he said. "We should be dead on."

At that moment both Buckee and Lewis, relaxing the intensity of their watch ahead, realized that they were alone on the water. Any craft now within two hundred yards would have shown up. There was nothing. The time was ten minutes past four. The coast of France was perhaps four miles ahead. Fifty minutes to zero.

Both Buckee and Lewis had studied Belleville Beach in all its known aspects until they knew the shape and slope of its shingle, its boulders, and its wave-cut rock, like the palms of their hands. The whole extent of the beach was barely one hundred yards. There was a footpath leading away from the beach up a narrow defile. That defile would show up as a gap in the line of cliffs, and would lead them in. At any moment now they might hope to detect this small gap in the dark low line ahead.

"Get hold of Major Young," Buckee said.

Major Peter Young, M.C., of the Beds and Herts Regiment, in command of No. 6 Troop, had about him that same air of simplicity, almost of innocence, that was a characteristic of Buckee and Lewis. War had enhanced this aspect of their natures. They had become dedicated, a part of war, and the normal questionings and complexities of their thoughts, even of their ambitions, had fallen away from them.

Lt. Buckee had remained for a short while alone peering at the low dark shelf of the land for the first sign of the break in its solid form that would give him his direct course. Major Young had come to stand beside him in silence waiting for the naval lieutenant to speak. Both men were curiously at ease.

"We are alone," Buckee said. He paused for a moment, not for effect, but simply to strip what he had to say of all pomposity and arrogance. He was the Captain of this small vessel, and he knew quite clearly what he must and would do.

"My orders are very clear," he said. "They are to land my detachment of troops, and to run aground if necessary to do so."

Major Young replied with the same unforced yet grave formality.

"My orders are equally clear: we are to go ashore whatever happens."

"We'll get you in on time," said Buckee, and both men began to feel the blood running in them with a sense of rising excitement, almost of exaltation, and presently this sense gripped the whole complement of the small craft binding them in that comradeship peculiar to danger.

Sub.-Lt. Lewis kept close watch for the first sign of the gap in the cliffs that would lead them to their target while Buckee and Peter Young held a brief Council of War. They were young men, but in this business of war they were already old. There were three officers and seventeen men in the headquarters party aboard the landing craft. It would not be possible to leave a bridgehead contingent. Buckee would stand offshore, taking all the evasive action he could if he came under fire. But it was clear to both men that with the best will in the world, and all the ingenuity known to man, the landing craft might be forced to withdraw.

"If you have to get away," Peter Young said, "don't worry. We'll make our way through to Dieppe."

That might be the wisest course. Dieppe was not more than three miles by the coast road, and distance could not be measured in miles. Three hundred yards or so back to the beach might easily have become more deadly than three miles inland. It could be less, if they joined up with the Royal Regiment at Puits.

When these swift and simple decisions had been reached Lt. Buckee forged ahead. The gap in the cliffs was clear now, a narrow cleft running up out of the darkness of the strip of beach at Belleville.

"Yellow two!" said Buckee. "Stand by to land."

Major Young, his two officers, Captain Selwyn of the 13th/18th Hussars and Lt. A. F. Ruxton, and seventeen men, who would follow him willingly ashore, looked carefully to their weapons. They were meagre. Between them they mustered: 1 Garrard rifle, 9 service rifles, 1 Bren gun, 6 tommy-guns, 3 pistols, 1 two-inch mortar with 6 bombs, 1 three-inch mortar with 4 bombs.

With these men and these weapons Major Peter Young was resolved to attack the Goebbels battery. He had no grandiose ideas in his head. Between them they would improvise, and do the best they could.

At precisely fifteen minutes to five o'clock, five minutes before zero in the Nautical Twilight, Lt. Buckee ran his vessel in within fifty yards of the spot he had selected for himself on his map. They were slightly to the right of the beach. There were no sounds beyond the crunch of shingle and the soft wash of the sea.

Quietly, unseen and unopposed, Major Young led his party swiftly over the sloping shingle to the dark shelter of the cliffs. He, too, knew the pattern of this little beach like the palm of his hand. For a short while Lt. Buckee, with his second-in-command Sub-Lt. Lewis by his side, watched the small party disappear in silence. There was in those first few minutes a remarkable peace.

Then Buckee began to draw his landing craft away from the
beach. It was already dawn, and the last cover of the night had
gone.

2

It took Major Young's men rather more than half an hour to
get off the narrow shelving beach of Belleville. Moving swiftly
over the heavy shingle, acutely aware of the crunch of boots on
the slippery rounded stones, they reached the entrance to the
narrow steep-sided gully that was the only outlet. At first sight it
looked impassable. The Germans had done an elaborate and
painstaking job with barbed and rabbit wire, filling the whole
gully to a depth of about seven feet. The barbed wire was stretched
very taut and pinioned to iron stakes driven into the sides of the
gully. The long barbs of the wire were not more than an inch
apart.

For a seemingly interminable five minutes the small party
felt trapped as they sought a way up, over or round the obstacle.
They had not a pair of wire cutters between them, nor was there a
Bangalore torpedo. This kind of thing had not been their role.
From the silence and the deserted feel of the beach it seemed
evident that the Germans discounted a serious threat from this
point. It was probable, too, that there were mines and booby traps.

Major Young and Lt. Ruxton explored warily. The iron stakes
driven into the sides of the gully extended about five feet out of
the ground, and they found that it was just possible to gain foot
and hand holds. They were greatly helped over the worst parts
of the climb by a rope fashioned quickly from some ends of
toggle ropes by Driver J. Cunningham of the R.A.S.C.

In all this silent laboured struggle the three-inch mortar had
to be abandoned on the beach. Two men could not work together
over that awkward climb, and the heavy weapon was too much for
one man to handle.

All the time as they made the climb the noises of battle grew in
their ears to the westward, while they felt themselves exposed
like so many winkles on pins to the marksman who might be
waiting his moment to pick them off. Two Bostons coming in low
from the sea to bomb the Goebbels battery drew a terrific barrage

of anti-aircraft fire from the neighbouring cliffs of Berneval. But the sight heartened them, as the aircraft came straight in on their target, and then soared away in high curving arcs to safety.

The silence of the battery at this time seemed very strange. A much more swift reaction had been expected, and it would have been a great help to the airmen in spotting their targets.

Major Young had felt sure that the naval action must have alerted the defenders of this piece of coast, yet now, a good half-hour after zero on the flanks, there was, it seemed, little or no knowledge of the assaults that should be going in all along the line from Puits to the River Saane at Quiberville. Indeed it was impossible to mistake the avalanche of fire that was rising to a fearful crescendo away to their right.

At last at the cliff top and over the wire the small party saw five landing craft coming straight in to Yellow Beach One in the light of the morning, and almost at once a hail of fire lashed the water as though the arrival of the craft had detonated an explosion. Covering the landing craft was the Motor Launch 346, blazing away with her whole armament of three-pounder, Lewis guns and Oerlikons. The sight tore at the hearts and throats of the watchers, and it was almost impossible not to watch in fascination as this spectacle developed. The odds were great, and coming in·on the flank to harass the solitary motor launch was a German ship of about two hundred tons.

The time was just after a quarter past five o'clock. It was a sight both brave and terrible as the five landing craft grounded and the motor launch turned her three-pounder on the German craft.

The sloping shingle beach of Berneval was a good four hundred yards wide. On the cliff top there were several houses and one building with the look of a church, and from a score of points deadly streams of fire concentrated on the very few who had gained the beach. But on the cliffs of Belleville the small party dared not pause. Major Young split his men into four groups. There could not be a definite plan of action against the powerful battery. They would have to improvise, but it was clear that from first to last they must strive to disguise their numbers from the enemy, and contrive to convey an impression of some strength. To do this they would have to harass the battery with all the fire they could bring to bear from as many points of the compass as possible. They must move fast and shoot fast, darting from cover to cover. Without the three-inch mortar they could not hope, even by a near miracle, to administer a *coup de grâce*: they could hope only to harass, but they must harass like a swarm of angry wasps.

The outline of a rough plan was quickly given as the party lay in a strip of woodland by the road that leads from Dieppe to Berneval, and at once Peter Young went forward alone to spy out the ground towards Berneval village. He was in luck. Coming along the road was a boy on a bicycle, a lad of about sixteen, pedalling fast towards Berneval as though pursued by the devil. The boy slewed his bike to a standstill as Major Young stood up in front of him, and the joy and excitement that chased the fear and shock from the boy's face were better than words. The English were welcome with this first young Frenchman, and at once the boy began to give the best way of approach to the Goebbels battery. There was a garrison of about two hundred men, he said, and all within a close perimeter of wire.

Major Young whistled up his men and they followed at the double as the boy led them into Berneval. The sounds of the early morning gunfire out to sea had aroused the villagers before the dawn, and now with the harsh stutter of machine-guns and the furious crump of mortars weaving the thunder of heavier guns into a hideous pattern, a score or more of young men rushed out to greet the small band of British. It was heartening, but the situation was one of extreme urgency. From out of that terrible din thickening within the narrow confines of Yellow Beach One no reinforcements would come.

Six Hurricanes swooping in low level attack against the Goebbels battery created an Heaven-sent diversion as Young's party cut the telephone wires to Dieppe, and spread out swiftly through the village. Up to this point not a single shot had been fired at them, but a burst of light machine-gun fire forced them to cover as they came abreast of the village church. Private Adderton of the Beds and Herts Regiment located the fire almost at once. The machine-gun was in the church tower, and Private Adderton returned the fire with his pistol, his only weapon, until Capt. Selwyn and Lt. Ruxton came in with their tommy-guns, and the two-inch mortar was set up. The first mortar bomb silenced the enemy, and the group rushed forward in an attempt to climb the church tower and gain a fine sniping position for their own Bren.

But there were no steps or stairs, and no time to be lost. Already Major Young had led off out of the village and through a small orchard with no worse obstacle than a dummy machine-gun post. Once out of the orchard there was precious little cover, and there was nothing for it but to spread out and run the gauntlet of sniping across a cornfield. Thanks to the villagers they knew the best approach to the battery, and using patches of scrub all four groups well spread out crawled unseen to within two hundred yards of the perimeter wire.

It was nearly half past six o'clock when Major Young's men opened fire from four points on the battery. By then they knew in their hearts beyond a doubt that they faced the task alone. But they were not quite alone. Whatever fate had befallen their comrades of No. 3 Commando striving to land in daylight against hopeless odds on the Berneval beach, it was uncomfortably plain that the motor launch was still in the fight. Her three-pounder gun, ranging now on the Goebbels battery, harassed Young's men as they sought to creep up almost under the enemy wire. But the efforts of the motor launch were a heartening diversion, helping far more than they hindered. Moving swiftly from point to point in a growing rhythm the four groups of lightly armed men sniped the battery with a kind of remorseless and inspired energy, never giving themselves away, and finally driving the enemy to such a pitch of frustration that one of the 5.9-inch guns of the battery was turned upon them. It gave them all very queer feelings as they watched the barrel of the big gun depressed as low as it would go, and seeming to point straight at them, but they clung close to the ground, held their own fire, and kept their heads. They knew they were safely under the trajectory as the powerful weapon, with its role of defending the seas off Dieppe, sent its shells harmlessly over the heads of the attackers almost under its muzzle.

Again and again as the 5.9. belched its fire the whole party concentrated their fire power into the clouds of yellow and black smoke pouring from the gun mouth.

This extraordinary tactic was a measure of the enemy's anxiety, but Major Young was determined not to overplay his hand. He knew that once his weakness was suspect the enemy would abandon his remarkable caution. At any time an enemy sortie in platoon strength would force the small British group to run for it, and perhaps make their escape from Belleville impossible.

Every minute, as the enemy fire became more concentrated, it was increasingly difficult for so few men to maintain the speed of movement essential to an effective fire-pattern. All their ears and senses were attuned to detect signs of change in the situation. Before half past seven o'clock the battle on Berneval beach had almost died away, and the enemy must guess the true picture of events.

A few minutes before half past seven o'clock Major Young sent off Capt. Selwyn alone to regain the beach at Belleville, to find out if by some miracle the landing craft of Lt. Buckee had contrived to stand by. If so Capt. Selwyn was to fire three white Very lights. Otherwise they would attempt to get through to Puits or Dieppe, and hope that the whole coast was not by now swarming with enemy.

Fifteen minutes later the three white Very lights hung their message above Belleville. At precisely twenty-three minutes to seven o'clock Lt. Buckee was bringing his craft in as calmly and coolly as on an exercise.

Even then Major Young held the withdrawal to a dignified pace, each man firing steadily as the enemy, at last venturing from his defences, followed at a respectful distance. But at the last the small party were in grave danger, and Major Young and Lt. Ruxton held the pass to the beach while the men got back over the wire. In an attempt to regain the three-inch mortar L/Cpl. White trod on a mine, but he struggled on, and before Young and Ruxton reached the beach the badly wounded man had his mortar in action, getting off all his bombs against the battery.

The time was now nearly eight o'clock as Buckee, covered by the motor launch, which had been in continuous action for more than two and a half hours, brought his craft in to the rescue. He had manœuvred his vessel with the utmost skill and resource using smoke-screens and under sustained enemy fire almost from the moment of putting the men on shore.

There was now no time to lose. The enemy were pressing close on the beachhead and but for the furious covering fire of the launch the whole party might have been wiped out as they waded through the shallows in the ebbing tide. L/Cpl. White was safely through helped by his mates. Lt. Ruxton, floating the Bren gun on his Mae West, pushed it ahead of him, with Trooper Abbott, the Bren gunner, wading at his side. Only then did Major Young see fit to leave Yellow Beach Two.

At ten minutes past eight the whole party were safely on board, and laying a last smoke-screen as the enemy blazed away fiercely from the cliffs, Lt. Buckee steered for England with the motor launch covering him.

For one and a half hours throughout all the critical period of the main landings these few men had succeeded in crippling the Goebbels battery, and preventing it from fulfilling its role effectively.

3

An hour before Lt. Buckee got under way from Belleville a single landing craft with a handful of survivors had limped slowly out to sea from Yellow Beach One. Of the six L.C.P.'s that had finally landed their troops on Berneval beach she was the only one to escape. Even so little seemed a miracle.

There had been no doubts in the minds of any of the men manning these small ships when, more than an hour before first light, they had found themselves alone in the darkness, their leader gone. Five out of six had rallied round the searching motor launch, not alone by chance, but by determination and good seamanship. The sixth, losing all contact with her neighbours, finally pressed on alone to reach Berneval some twenty minutes after the leaders. Simply, all these men had gone forward with high hearts to try to wrest triumph from disaster.

Seldom, if ever, had men been so well briefed in their parts. They all knew that the Goebbels battery must be silenced, and for all they could know they were all that remained of the powerful Group 5. The task had become their own, and all hope of that surprise, considered vital to success, had been lost in the growing light of day.

At fifteen minutes past five o'clock, twenty-five minutes late, and covered by the motor launch, herself a David defying a Goliath, Lt.-Commander C. L. Corke, R.N.V.R., and Lt. D. R. Stephens, R.N.V.R., of the 2nd and 24th flotillas, led in the five landing craft to Yellow One.

It seemed almost that they must be invisible from the shore as the sea narrowed and the beach came forward to meet them. A large white house with the church-like building nearby stood out clearly on the cliff top. A bare quarter of a mile beyond lay the Goebbels battery that was their goal. There was no sound, no sign of movement in all that small amphitheatre of rounded stones.

But there were no illusions aboard the small craft coming so steadily in to land in that silence that smelled of doom. The men searched the stretch of beach with eyes that burned like lamps in the hot masks of their set faces, and betrayed the high pitched key of their senses. From the groyne near by the eastern defile to the boulders merging into the rock westward, this was the piece of earth they had studied so long and carefully. It was exactly as they had expected, but in this there was no reassurance. They knew even the shape and size of its flint stones. They knew also many of its secrets, and that these innocent-seeming cliffs held machine-gun posts and cunningly concealed pill-boxes.

At low water springs this narrow strip of steeply sloping shingle that stood between the cliffs and the sea would widen to a good three hundred yards. If they endured while the tide ebbed that fact would be of great importance, but time had narrowed down now to a moment of truth that stood isolated from all that had gone before, or might come after. Thus these men of No. 3 Commando braced themselves for the ordeal of the final gauntlet.

In the end it was as though the landing craft released some hidden spring to touch off an explosion that engulfed them upon the instant in a shuddering chaos of ships and men. That first appalling impact of enemy fire denied the survival of the living flesh, and in that moment of touching down the wounded lay in the grotesque embraces of those struck dead in the last postures of living.

But ships and men came on. One man replaced another in the quickening rhythm of tragedy that drew this small band of men steadily into its diminishing pattern. As Lt.-Commander Corke and his boatswain fell mortally wounded side by side, a commando trooper took the wheel and landed those who survived as the craft sank under them.

Those who reached the shingle pressed on almost blindly, unable in that fearful spasm to locate the fire against them. But the motor launch, harassed as she was almost at the outset by the armed German tanker *Franz* coming in against her, at once observed the great volume of fire coming from the white house and the neighbouring church-like building on the cliffs, and her twin Oerlikons and Lewis guns were in instant action.

All that had been hidden was revealed at once by the stabbing bursts of flame and the slow lazy trajectory of tracer, as heavy and light machine-guns, mortars and snipers enfiladed the men leaping to the shingle and charging up that steep beach of stones. Even in that inferno of fire there were some who seemed to bear charmed lives, and others who, for a stride or two, appeared unharmed, even as their clothing smouldered in their wounds. The first man to land was Capt. R. L. Wills, of the Duke of Cornwall's Light Infantry. He was in the bows of the leading landing craft and had become the senior officer of all that remained of the Commando. Realizing that the only hope lay in speed and purpose he led his men in a direct charge for a short section of the wire and cut a way through, hoping to blaze a trail for those who might follow. By his side Corporal Halls of the same regiment charged like a man berserk, hurling grenades with such accuracy that he captured a machine-gun post single-handed. A short distance to his right Lt. Loustalot, one of the very few of the U.S. Rangers to get ashore, dashed forward under withering fire and died like a man clutching an armful of enemy spears to his body so that others might follow.

But for this bold leadership it is unlikely that a single man would have gained the cliffs. As it was, a handful of men with Capt. Wills reached the cliffs and at once began a spirited attack against the half-concealed enemy positions, hoping thereby to give some covering fire to those struggling across the beach. The task was hopeless. Wills himself was hit through the throat in the first minutes, able only to struggle back to the beach and to know no more. The beach now was littered with dead and dying men, but the fight was not yet lost. With a courage that seemed sublime the sixth landing craft, having found its way alone to the rendezvous, came steadily in to land with the guns of the motor launch covering her with magnificent effect. The motor launch, concentrating her fire on the white house and the church-like building, succeeded in silencing the enemy guns. A moment later both buildings were seen to be in flames.

In that brief respite those few on board the sixth landing craft rushed the shingle to add their numbers to the dead, and a precious few to those who fought and fired from under the cliffs.

At the same time the naval survivors on the landing craft were striving to manœuvre their vessels offshore with some of the wounded. The enemy fire had abated its first concentrated fury, not only by the loss of the gun positions in the cliff houses, but also by the spread of its targets. But it was no more than a lull in a storm that must swell to an even greater force as more and more mortars began to come in.

Somehow through all this the motor launch had held the German armed tanker *Franz* at bay, resisting the tanker's attempt to drive her inshore to her destruction, and refusing to turn her main armament away from the cover of the troops. But now the launch turned full upon the German, closing to thirty yards and overwhelming the tanker with the speed and devastating point-blank fire of the onslaught. Within ten minutes the tanker *Franz* ran aground in flames.

The time was fifteen minutes to six o'clock. With wonderful courage and calmness the sailors had transferred the wounded from the sunken landing craft in which Lt.-Commander Corke and his boatswain lay dead, and had contrived to withdraw the remaining vessels some way offshore. And there they waited, ready to go in again to land on a signal from the small naval beach party on shore.

For more than one and a half hours until seven o'clock the nameless brave on that beach, by defying overwhelming odds and holding the enemy in increasing strength with his face to the sea, must have aided the twenty men of their commando who, unknown to them, harried the Goebbels battery from the rear.

At sea the motor launch, while never abating the accuracy and intensity of her fire, and even harassing the Goebbels battery with her three-pounder shells, had gained some tangible emblems of her swift victory over the German armed tanker. A boarding party had brought off the enemy ensign and trophies.

A few minutes before seven o'clock it became clear that the end was not far off. The firing from under the cliffs had almost died away, and the Germans were now attacking almost every inch of the beach with mortars and grenades. Even under the cliffs there was no cover. If any man remained alive to be saved

46

it was now or never, and the crews of the five landing craft came in again to land.

But a new hazard had arisen with the ebbing tide. Steel stakes about four or five feet long had been driven into the beach in rows extending seaward and these now sprouted above the water. Only three of the landing craft succeeded in overcoming these obstacles and getting in at all. Of these three, one went aground on the rocks, and the other stuck fast on the steel stakes.

Somehow a few of the naval beach party had survived on that deadly stretch of shingle and the last remaining landing craft took them on board as they swam out under a hail of fire. No soldiers could be seen; no answering fire could be discerned in all that web of sound; and as though to confirm the totality of death the enemy turned the full force of his fire upon the three small targets on the rim of the sea.

It seemed impossible then for the last landing craft afloat to go to the aid of those still living upon the other two stranded vessels. That small plot of sea between seethed with bullets like a boiling cauldron, yet heedless of it all Leading Signalman Coggeshall took to the water with a line in an attempt to reach his mates. Barely five minutes earlier he had himself been rescued from the beach.

The landing craft on the rocks was by now in flames, but Coggeshall reached the vessel pinioned on the steel stakes and made his line fast. For a second or two it seemed that a miracle might happen, and then the towing-post came adrift under the strain. The last landing craft had now become the very core of a tornado of fire that seemed to bounce her like a cork as Coggeshall and the last naval survivors took to the water and somehow regained her meagre shelter.

But for the intense covering fire of the motor launch it seems that they must have failed. She had come dangerously close inshore to be attendant upon this last rite of rescue. With that accuracy and inspiration which she had sustained from the outset, the motor launch,[1] concentrated every weapon she had aboard against the enemy gun posts, as the last landing craft backed away from Yellow Beach One, and slowly out to sea.

[1] M.L. 346.

CHAPTER FIVE

SIX O'CLOCK

AT THIS hour all that was clearly known aboard the Headquarters ship *Calpe* was that the operation was not going according to plan. More than ninety per cent of the force had been committed, and in the main there was little to do but wait.

To mask the main landings Blenheims had laid a curtain of smoke over the formidable East headland, Bismarck, which dominated the Dieppe beaches. Now, at six o'clock, as the last veils of smoke were blown away in the freshening wind the gun-boat, H.M.S. *Locust*, steamed for the 330-feet-wide entrance between the two dog-leg converging jetties of the outer harbour of Dieppe. This was the last of the planned assaults. Behind *Locust*, poised in complete readiness, the Fighting French Chasseurs with the Royal Marine Commando awaited the signal that would send them through that narrow gap to seize the invasion barges and make a havoc of the docks. The signal did not come. At once, as the smoke cleared, the hidden batteries in the recesses of the Bismarck headland attacked *Locust* with an over-whelming weight of fire. The gunboat replied with all her fire-power, but within five minutes she was twice badly hit, and power-less against the headland fortress.

H.M.S. *Locust* could not hope to shoot her way through: her task was hopeless.

The destroyers *Albrighton* and *Berkeley*, together with *Calpe* and *Fernie*, were already plastering the East headland while striving to cover the men who should, by this time, be off the beaches. But it was soon apparent that the fire-power of the destroyers was hopelessly inadequate. At ten minutes past six o'clock H.M.S. *Locust* withdrew reluctantly from the harbour gateway, rather than become a useless sacrifice.

These things; the tremendous fire-power brought to bear on the attackers not only from the Bismarck headland, but from the Rommel, Hitler and Goering batteries behind the beaches, told a dismal story to the Naval and Military Force Commanders.

From the Yellow Beaches there had been no word at all. From

48

the Blue Beach at Puits had come only the news that the Royal Regiment of Canada had landed seventeen minutes late: that is, at seven minutes past five o'clock. That news alone was cold comfort, and the rest was silence. More than an hour had passed and the Bismarck headland and the Rommel batteries, the first vital objectives of that attack, were pounding out the evidence of their powerful condition.

From the western flank the first news was more promising. No. 4 Commando had gone in exactly on time, achieving surprise on the beaches of Vasterival and Quiberville. On the Green Beach of Pourville things were thought to be developing 'not unfavourably' for the South Saskatchewan Regiment, and behind them the Queen's Own Cameron Highlanders of Canada had got ashore under heavy fire.

In the main it was a bald cold picture leaving too much to the imagination, and constantly confused by messages that were gravely suspect. Even the course of events on the Red and White Beaches of Dieppe was almost completely obscure. Poor visibility together with the smoke-screens made visual observation impossible. The Essex Scottish Regiment and the Royal Hamilton Light Infantry had landed on time. The tanks should by now be up and over the esplanade. The Royal Canadian Engineers should be detonating their many charges.

Two waves of tanks had gone in. At five minutes to six o'clock a message had been received from Brigadier Lett on board a tank landing craft of the second wave:

"We are about to land."

A similar message had come from Lt.-Colonel Andrews, commanding the 14th Canadian Army Tank Battalion. (The Calgary Regiment), and flying his pennant from his tank carried on Tank Landing Craft 125.

After that, only silence.

The first wave of tanks had touched down five minutes late.

As the *Calpe* was brilliantly handled in that now turbulent area of sea, skilfully sheltering the stream of returning landing craft that were coming alongside with their sparse news and their wounded, the Military and Naval Force Commanders waited anxiously for something hard, something that would guide them to a course of action. For an hour the smoke from the burning buildings along the Dieppe front, the smoke-screens laid by aircraft and destroyers, had added to the difficulties of direct vision, and it seemed that the whole elaborate system of wireless communication from shore to ship had virtually broken down.

The one unescapable fact was that the East headland, Bismarck, was nothing short of a natural fortress weaving a deadly pattern of fire over all that seventeen-hundred-yard-long stretch of the Dieppe beaches, and also out to sea. The main secrets of the headland had defied the eyes of the cameras even on the last very daring low-level air sorties. Its power had been grossly under-estimated. Guns of high calibre, probably 88's and French 75's, were firing with great speed and accuracy. They were also invisible, and it seemed invulnerable.

But even in the obscurity of that hour decisions had to be taken for better or worse. At half past six o'clock the Force Commanders held a conference aboard *Calpe* with Commander R. E. D. Ryder, V.C., R.N., of H.M.S. *Locust*. They had to decide one urgent question:

Was it feasible to carry on with the entry into Dieppe Harbour, the dock demolitions and the cutting-out operation?

Within a few minutes the inevitable was faced and the project was abandoned. This was primarily a naval decision, but it was of the greatest importance to Major-General Roberts for it released the powerful Royal Marine Commando at once to come under his command, and with the Fusiliers Mont-Royal doubled the strength of his floating reserve. The third wave of tanks was also waiting off-shore for orders.

It was now the turn of the Military Force Commander to act. The outstanding necessity was to secure the East headland 'at all costs'. By this time the naval forces were themselves under continuous fire, manœuvring behind smoke-screens, taking evasive action from the menace of the air battle as well as of the shore batteries, and with their guns in incessant action. It was not a simple matter to form a judgment on the pattern of fire on shore, but it did seem that the weight of fire directed against Red Beach was diminishing.

It seemed then to Major-General Roberts that more infantry were needed, if any success there might be could be exploited. Accordingly the Fusiliers Mont-Royal were ordered in at once to land under all the cover of smoke and fire that could be brought to bear from sea and air. Behind them the Royal Marines transhipped from the Chasseurs to landing craft to await their new role, whatever it might be.

These operations, and many others of considerable difficulty, were being performed at sea with perfect smoothness in circumstances of growing danger and difficulty. Soon after six o'clock one of the flak landing craft, equipped as a medical ship, had been badly hit and her medical staff, together with all the wounded, had taken to the water. Both *Calpe* and *Fernie* were taking on board all the wounded they could accommodate and the numbers of wounded were growing steadily, though not out of hand. Meanwhile a Boat Pool was formed for all craft returning from their various roles, and all held in instant readiness to embark on new tasks.

The R.A.F. co-operation from the moment of the initial flanking attacks against the Pointe D'Ailly light to the West and the Goebbels battery to the East had not been short of perfection. Indeed the squadrons were doing more than had been planned and promised. Nevertheless the war in the air over Dieppe was not developing in the way Air Marshal Leigh-Mallory had hoped. His determination to lure the entire German Air Force in the West into the air seemed unlikely of fulfilment. The R.A.F. wanted a show-down that would underline the lesson of the Battle of Britain, but the German Air Force was being unconscionably slow to react. At fifteen minutes past five o'clock the first Spitfires and Bostons had gone in, and from that moment the air pattern had developed swiftly, attack after attack going in against the Rommel, Hitler and Goering batteries behind the central beaches. In great daring the squadrons had supported the main landings, and the fortified hotels and boarding houses on the front of Dieppe had been in flames as the first attacks from the sea went in.

Despite all that there were not more than thirty F.W. 190's in the air against the R.A.F. more than an hour later. They had expected many more: they were furious for more. And now, as the first specific demands began to reach No. 11 Group Headquarters from Air Commodore Cole aboard H.M.S. *Calpe* the R.A.F. tried to meet them with enthusiasm. At fifteen minutes to seven o'clock every available Boston of 88 Squadron was ordered to attack the Rommel battery behind Puits, while new sorties went in against the Hitler and Goering batteries. These batteries were firing with great steadiness in spite of consistent fierce low-level air attacks, and it was already very clear that the combined fire-power of the destroyers was unequal to the task of making an impression against the heavier shore defences which had the added advantage of the accuracy of firing from fixed positions.

But one thing Major-General Roberts wanted at that hour of the landing of the Fusiliers Mont-Royal was smoke over the Bismarck headland, and he could not get it at such short notice. All the smoke-carrying aircraft were already on their way to pre-arranged targets, and it would be more than an hour before any more could be bombed up. Instead, as the twenty-six unarmoured landing craft carrying the Fusiliers Mont-Royal to the beaches emerged from the smoke-screens laid by the destroyers, a squadron of Hurricane cannon fighters dived in against the headland.

So the Force Commanders waited aboard *Calpe* and *Fernie* while their A/A gunners poured shells into the sky against the first fighter attacks, and the dog fights for which the Spitfires and Hurricanes hungered wove their patterns in the clouding sky.

There had been no further word from Brigadier Lett or Lt.-Colonel Andrews, and the third and fourth waves of tanks still waited for the word of command that would send them in. These and the Royal Marines were the last cards Major-General Roberts held. He might have to play them blind.

The first news of the landings in the Dieppe area had reached German G.H.Q. West at half past six o'clock. The last entry in their record at this time was:

'0650 hours—Situation still unclear.'

No orders had been given to the 10th Panzer Division or to the Adolf Hitler S.S. Division in the area. Nor were they alerted. No movement of enemy troops was discernible from the air despite the very daring sorties flown by the reconnaissance Mustangs.

But time was on their side.

CHAPTER SIX

THE ORANGE BEACHES

I

THE two hundred and fifty officers and men of No. 4 Commando
under Lt.-Colonel The Lord Lovat, M.C., had transhipped into
their landing craft from the Infantry Landing Ship *Prince
Albert*, exactly at the appointed hour of three o'clock. Without
the semblance of a hitch the landing craft had then formed two
columns in convoy under the command of Lt.-Commander
H. H. H. Mulleneux, R.N., on board the Motor Gun Boat 312.
These with the Steam Gun Boat 9 comprised Group 1.

With the Commander's motor gun boat leading on the port
beam the landing craft, keeping station as though in the light of
day, sailed steadily on their course for the Orange Beaches of
Vasterival and Quiberville. The destroyers *Bleasdale*, *Albrighton*,
Berkeley and *Garth*, at this stage, screened their western flank.
They felt secure. They had, even then, that sense of riding the tide
that leads on to victory.

The star shells, heralding the naval action on the extreme
left flank, and the sustained fire of that brief engagement, brought
them no forebodings. If anything it keened the edge of alertness
on board the motor gun boat. To the men in the landing craft
it came as something of a relief in the long silence of the run-
in, for most of them had already endured some of these long
silences of which the end is very often sound and fury, and
death.

It was soon apparent to Mulleneux that whatever was happen-
ing away on the left flank the equanimity of the enemy ashore
seemed undisturbed. On his port quarter he could make out the
wink of the Dieppe Harbour light, and this might mean either a
complete lack of suspicion or the likely presence of enemy ships
bound for Dieppe. Or both. At any rate, it was reassuring. Fine
on his starboard bow the Pointe d'Ailly light, high on the headland
dividing the Orange Beaches on which his two columns must land,
continued to flash its normal characteristic. It augured well. The

Pointe d'Ailly light was a beacon to lead them in, but it also made Mulleneux 'smell' enemy shipping.

Almost at that moment when the Steam Gun Boat 5 wallowed to a standstill with her guns silenced and her boilers holed eleven miles to the East off Berneval, Mulleneux spotted three darkened shapes dead ahead. They were about three miles off-shore; enemy ships East-bound, feeling their way towards Dieppe.

Instantly the Commander altered course to starboard and reduced speed to 7 knots, while the convoy slid round the tail of the enemy with not so much as a creak of boots or a muffled cough from the men aboard to betray their presence. Unalarmed the enemy ships steamed on their course and two minutes later the motor gun boat resumed her true course and steered for the Pointe d'Ailly light.

These happenings had served to bring every man to a pitch of anticipation as the landing craft in their two-column formation diverged for their beaches. The smaller column held dead ahead for Vasterival, Orange Beach One, while the larger aimed at a point to the west of the headland light to come ashore as near as possible to where the Saane meets the sea. Both columns were dead on time. The wail of air-raid sirens from the shore came eerily over the water, a welcome sound promising that the Spitfires were coming in with perfect timing for the first attack on the light-house, and to create a diversion as the landings went in. All was well.

The Hess battery was silent. It must mean that their presence, and the presence of the whole armada off Dieppe, was as yet unsuspected. At this hour the powerful Groups 10, 11 and 12 would be moving in towards the Dieppe beaches, and easy game for the two flanking coastal batteries. The Hess battery could blow them all out of the water with the greatest of ease. It was zero hour in the Nautical Twilight.

2

The whole lay-out and strength of the Hess battery had been carefully translated from air photographs and other sources, and studied with meticulous care. Not only the power of the battery, but also many details of its defences were known to the officers and men of No. 4 Commando. They had worked out exactly what they had to do, and how they would do it.

The battery of six 15 cm. guns lay just behind the seaside village of Varengeville. Its special task was to put down a barrage in front of Dieppe at a range of 8,600 yards. On receipt of the order: 'Sperrfeuer Dieppe' six rounds per gun were to be fired.

These guns had been built for coastal defence in 1936 with a range of 23,800 yards. Together with the less powerful Goebbels battery they constituted the most important part of the Dieppe defences. Each of the guns was mounted on a concrete platform revolving on a central pivot. Five of the guns formed a single group while the sixth was placed at some little distance from the main battery, and with a 2 cm. anti-tank gun used also against aircraft. A 2 cm. A/A gun was also mounted on a tower immediately behind the main emplacement position, and a third 2 cm. gun was mounted on concrete slightly to the North-East of the battery; that is, slightly forward to seaward on the Dieppe side.

This whole formidable armament was defended against infantry attack by a double apron fence of wire all round the outer perimeter, and with seven machine-gun posts each manned by four or five men under a junior N.C.O. Two of these posts were of concrete.

To the South, inland, the machine-gun posts had magnificent fields of fire over two or three hundred yards of open country to belts of woodland. In addition a garrison up to five hundred men might be expected.

Lt.-Colonel The Lord Lovat, Major D. Mills Roberts of the Irish Guards, his officers and men had studied this difficult proposition with great care, and had made a plan to attack the battery from the front and rear. Major Mills Roberts, landing with C Troop, the 3-inch mortar and the mortar section, at Vasterival, Orange Beach One, would attack from the front, while the remainder of the Commando under Lovat would land as near to the East of the River Saane as possible at Quiberville, Orange Beach Two. While Major Mills Roberts and his party with the mortars engaged the enemy in a frontal attack, Lovat would move as fast as he possibly could in a detour round the flank to get into position to launch an assault from the rear.

The intention then was to carry the battery by storm, by the speed, fury and surprise of the attack from the rear. The Hess battery must not fire, at least after half past six o'clock that morning. On that they were resolved.

At ten minutes to five in the fading Nautical Twilight exactly on zero and with about two hundred yards' visibility the first flight of Lovat's men touched down and raced over the shingle for the cliffs of Quiberville. The enemy was there too, surprised but wideawake. Three minutes later Major Mills Roberts was ashore at Vasterival unseen, and at that moment cannon fighters of the Royal Air Force dived into the attack against the Pointe d'Ailly light. The timing was admirable.

3

Star shells were lighting the sky above the cliffs of Quiberville as Major Mills Roberts landed with C Troop on the boulder-strewn beach of Vasterival nearly a mile to the eastward. The star shells, followed at once by the burp of machine-guns and the harsh crump of mortars, warned C Troop grimly that the main body of the Commando were meeting a hot reception. Their own beach was silent, while half a mile to the west the cannon fighters dived upon the Pointe d'Ailly light in a flurry of A/A shell bursts. This diversion and their own good luck inspired C Troop. For the moment their arrival was unsuspected, and if they could move off the beach fast enough they would be able to dissolve into the woods that lay beyond the village of Varengeville, and from which they planned to launch their mortar attack.

Three gullies led off Vasterival, and up through one of them C Troop must go. While Major Mills Roberts got ashore and across the beach with the mortar section under command of Lt. J. F. Ennis, R.A., a sub-section of C Troop rushed ahead led by Lt. D. C. W. Style of the Lancs Fusiliers. They wasted no time. They found at once that the left-hand gully was virtually unscaleable, filled with a maze of wire woven into a deep labyrinth that would need patience and a great deal of explosive to deal with. They had not much of either to spare. Taking this in at a glance, Style moved across to the extreme right determined to blast a way through. That was the shortest route if they could make it. Without a moment's hesitation Style decided to use his Bangalore torpedoes to clear the wire, and to take the risk of alerting the enemy. It was the right choice and luck was with him. At the moment of explosion the cannon fighters made their last diving attack on the lighthouse and the anti-aircraft fire coupled with the noise of the cannon masked the din on Vasterival beach. Within five minutes the way was clear.

Followed by Capt. R. W. P. Dawson of the Loyals with another sub-section of the Troop, Style led on to Varengeville village. There was not even then a glimmer of light. Not a sentry challenged, and they caught the enemy literally with his boots off. Going swiftly from house to house, winkling out enemy, pacifying men, women and children, they made good their vital line of retreat to the beach bridgehead.

Meanwhile Major Mills Roberts with Lt. Ennis had moved very fast with the mortars to gain the cover of a thick wood with its forward edge a bare hundred yards from the battery wire. Stealthily, and almost as soundlessly as Red Indians, the party moved forward through the woods with the two-inch and three-inch mortars, while behind them Lt. Style deployed his sub-section ready to attack the enemy. Every man knew his part. Within half an hour of the landing C Troop seemed to have vanished without trace. The landing had passed entirely unnoticed by the enemy.

It was, in fact, extraordinarily peaceful. The firing had died down away to the west, and that seemed to augur well for Lovat's party. If all went well Lovat's attack should be ready to go in from the rear not a moment later than half past six o'clock. Until then C Troop must contrive to hold the enemy engaged from the front and, if possible, prevent the battery from performing its role.

By half past five the mortar section with the sub-section of Lt. Style had gained the forward boundary of the wood, and were able to work their way so close to the battery that they could hear clearly the words of commands to the gunners.

Major Mills Roberts held his fire. A belt of scrub lay between the woodland and the wire of the battery defences. It was far from thick, and nowhere on that piece of land could a man hope for cover from fire. But there was cover from view, and worming their ways foot by foot Lt. Style's men crawled forward. L/Cpl. Mann, a crack shot, knowing that some such role awaited him, had painted his hands and face green, and with this disguise he reached a clump of bushes from which he could pick off the enemy without the slightest danger of a miss. There he waited with his rifle ready. Gunner T. McDonough had managed with great patience to drag his heavy anti-tank rifle into a good forward position, while one of the mortar section had crawled to a small clump of bush in which he had contrived to make himself practically invisible. It was a fine O.P. for the mortars.

The battery had by now fired several salvoes, but it was clear that the order 'Sperrfeuer Dieppe' had not been given, and the enemy could not be fully alive to the position. The whole of Major Mills Roberts men had now reached the kind of positions they had planned and thought over as they had studied the air photographs and diagrams of all that piece of ground. They had also managed to locate a light machine-gun post on the roof of a near-by house. Their own Bren gun team had settled themselves comfortably, and from a score of points throughout that strip of scrub, within easy earshot of voices even in casual conversation, the marksmen of C Troop had selected their targets.

Until ten minutes to six o'clock Major Mills Roberts waited, and then at a signal every man opened up with devastating, but limited, effect. For a few minutes, at any rate, the enemy was off balance and scared, and C Troop knew well enough that they must try to carry this high note to breaking point.

Troop Sergeant-Major Dunning with Privates Dale and Horne had set up the two-inch mortar in a first-class position and had gauged the range perfectly. Their first shot was well on the target in the first moments of surprise. Almost at once the fire of C Troop had knocked out the light machine-gun on the house top, and even silenced two of the heavy machine-gun posts within the enemy wire.

The first bursts of enemy return fire were wild.

But these opening bars of the music of battle, for all their liveliness and effect, held no promise of the devastating chords that burst with appalling suddenness upon the battery and inspired the attackers to the heights of daring and exuberance. With the third two-inch mortar bomb Dunning and his team hit the cordite charges and the ammunition brought up from the magazines and stacked beside the guns ready for action. And with a blinding flash that seemed to lift men like paper in a whirlwind, the cordite blew up and the guns of the Hess battery were silenced at a single blow, never to fire again.

The time was exactly seven minutes past six o'clock. It was a *tour de force*.

Out of the blazing inferno at the heart of the battery in the aftermath of that awful blast came the screams of the wounded and the burned, as gunners and troops of the garrison ran wildly, in an attempt to fight the flames and save the guns. Into that bizarre and terrible scene C Troop directed its deadly fire.

As a battery the Hess position was no more, but as an enemy strong-point it was still a powerful and menacing proposition. There were perhaps four hundred enemy troops within the wire, and if once they found themselves they had it in their power to swat this small Commando party as easily as a man swats a fly. Knowing this full well C Troop strove with redoubled energy to keep the enemy off balance until Lovat's men were ready to go in against their heavily defended rear. Sergeant P. F. Macarthy with his Bren gunners was now reaping a grisly harvest as he raked the whole area of the flames with deadly bursts. L/Cpl. Mann had sniped throughout like a man possessed, while Gunner McDonough concentrated sixty rounds from his anti-tank rifle against the two flak towers. The three-inch mortar was now hurling its bombs steadily into the burning core of the battery position.

Yet it seemed certain that at any moment the enemy must make a desperate sortie in strength, to strike blindly through that slender strip of scrub that could not long conceal the small inspired band of the attackers. As the minutes ticked by to the planned timing of Lovat's assault the suspense grew. For perhaps thirty or forty more minutes the bridgehead might hold, but inevitably the trap must close behind them. C Troop's role was almost done.

At twenty minutes past six o'clock, exactly half an hour after Major Mills Roberts had opened his attack, three white Very lights rose beyond the battery. It was Lovat's signal for the assault, and at once at this welcome sight the three-inch mortar got off ten smoke bombs in quick succession. Swiftly, yet keeping under cover as much as they could, C Troop then began their withdrawal to the beachhead.

Their battle was won, even beyond their dreams, but the small party was not yet out of the wood. These were the minutes of greatest danger. Relieved from that deadly sniping the enemy mortars came rapidly into action ranged on the lines of retreat the troop must follow, and within a few minutes the enemy drew their first blood of revenge when a mortar burst killed one of Style's men on the edge of the wood. A moment later Style himself was badly wounded in the leg as he withdrew his sub-section round the left flank of the attack to gain the beach.

That was the total of the enemy's revenge. Limping and in pain, Style safely withdrew his men, while C Troop held open the escape route for Lord Lovat's party. Within two hours of their landing Major Mills Roberts and C Troop had left Orange Beach One almost as silently as they had come. The few salvoes fired by the Hess battery had not damaged a single craft of the groups moving in to the Red and White Beaches of Dieppe, nor had they caused anxiety to the destroyers.

4

Lord Lovat's landing had gone in with precision.

At ten minutes to five o'clock, exactly on the zero hour that had been so carefully planned, the leading landing craft carrying the first flight of No. 4 Commando slid in like ghosts over the quiet sea to the shingle bank of Quiberville beach and at the instant of touchdown Lt. A. S. S. Veasey leapt ashore with a strong fighter patrol of A Troop at his heels. These men had no illusions as they rushed that shingle bank to the dark line of the cliffs. For perhaps a minute or two the tactical surprise they had won by their magnificent timing might endure. In that brief lull they must drive home an advantage by the sheer speed and impetuosity of their charge and purpose. Upon them in great measure depended the lives of those who now must follow.

It was no part of Veasey's role to seek exits or to cast round for cover. He and every man behind him had been trained and blooded in the ways and means of desperate assault. That was their purpose.

As the warning star shells of the enemy climbed the twilit sky to alert that whole amphitheatre of war, Veasey and his men scaled the cliffs with tubular steel ladders, and were upon the forward defensive posts of the enemy before a shot could be fired. It was at that same moment that the cannon fighters of the R.A.F. dived in against the lighthouse still flashing from the point.

Grenades flung with deadly accuracy blasted the enemy from

cover. Two pill-boxes were overwhelmed. Here in all this heavily defended area of the Hess battery and the Pointe d'Ailly light the enemy was on his toes, yet unable to bring his strength to bear upon the Commando that had rushed so suddenly into his embrace.

It was a vital part of Veasey's role to cut communications, and to this end Trooper Finney rushed at once to the nearest telegraph pole as soon as he gained the cliff top. So alert was the enemy that before Finney had climbed three feet above the ground the machine-guns discovered him, and tore the pole to splinters under his hands. Yet Finney climbed on, seeming sheltered in a miraculous cocoon of invulnerability that at times enwraps the brave like a magic shield. The wires were singing with the wild violence of bullets as Finney reached the head of the pole, calmly performed his task, and slid down the shattered pole unscathed.

All this had happened in a matter of minutes, and while Veasey's men deployed to harry the enemy with all their power, the second wave of the Commando touched down close to the estuary of the Saane where the shingle gives way to sand. The whole line of the beach was spaced with wooden groynes, and it was as if the beach itself burst into eruption as the predicted fire of the enemy mortars came down upon the angles of the groynes, and the deep belts of wire between.

To the West, where the line of the River Saane gave a natural exit inland, the wire was worst and intense rifle and machine-gun and mortar fire came down upon the first men to reach a belt of wire fifteen feet deep. These few lay up close seeking to bridge the barbs with nets of rabbit wire, but four men died in the first bursts of machine-gun fire, and a moment later a mortar got the range and wiped out a sub-section of B Troop as they flung themselves upon the barrier.

This small disaster opened the way. In the act of dying these men had bridged the wire with the rabbit netting and their own bodies, and as the German mortar teams, elated with their success, turned their weapons upon the landing craft, Lovat rushed the wire with his main force and got across without another casualty.

Notices posted up in French to warn passers-by of land mines made the rest easy for these highly trained men, and in close formation the whole Commando followed Lovat at the double along the East bank of the Saane while their landing craft withdrew safely out to sea. But for the dead, Quiberville beach was deserted. By achieving tactical surprise and by the sheer speed of their assault, No. 4 Commando had carried the beach almost in their stride in the face of an alert enemy with the whole narrow terrain under his guns. A hold-up even of five minutes would have meant almost certain disaster.

One and all Lovat's men knew the River Saane, the woods that bordered it, the little farms, and all that piece of country with the Hess battery at its heart. For the best part of a mile they kept to the river bank before bearing left to gain the cover of Blancmenil-le-bas wood. It was in this wood with its northern edge facing the rear of the battery that Lovat had planned to reconnoitre concentration areas, and to make the assault upon the battery.

At this point the enemy had lost track of the Commando completely, and they had reached the wood unseen. From the moment of leaving the vicinity of the beach not a shot had been fired, and within an hour of landing the Commando were concentrated in the wood, baffling the enemy completely by the speed and scope of their detour. So unaware were the Germans of danger from the rear that a body of Stosstruppe, thirty-five men strong, forming up behind a farmhouse ready to attack Major Mills Roberts party, were caught off balance by F Troop of Lovat's force and wiped out to a man with tommy-gun fire, as though blindfold they faced a firing squad.

At once in the wood Lovat divided his force into two troops while fighter patrols went forward with Bangalore torpedoes to crawl upon the enemy wire and prepare to breach the first line of outer defence. The plan was simple. The two troops would charge the battery from two points simultaneously and carry the defences at all costs.

The lively opening fire of Major Mills' party came to their ears like sweet music with the crump of the mortar bombs and the men of the fighter patrols were already almost on the wire with their Bangalore torpedoes as the great roar of the exploding cordite shook the earth. That appalling detonation, followed by the sheet of flame which sprang in a livid flash from the heart of the battery, was a cover and an inspiration to the men of B and F Troops as they lay, tensed for action, on the forward boundaries of the woodland staring over nearly three hundred yards of open ground to the battery perimeter. They were almost ready.

Half a dozen men of the U.S. Rangers, almost all of that small token group to get ashore on either flank, but for the brave Loustalot on Yellow One, had worked their way meanwhile to flanking positions. Two U.S. sergeants, together with Corporal F. Koons, had gained entry to houses and climbed to roof-tops overlooking the battery.

By a quarter past six o'clock the stage was set, and every man was in his place. They knew that the sands must be running out for the brave show C Troop were putting up with unabated vigour from the North. Thus they awaited the cannon fighters of the R.A.F. due to go in against the battery and signal by their arrival the moment of zero. Right on time, harassed by F.W. 190's of the enemy, the cannon fighters came swooping and swerving out of the clouding sky and at their coming twin streams of men with bayonets fixed surged like a tide over that open ground.

A fragment of the splendour in the terrible drama of war was caught in that moment of climax as the cannon fighters dived and the smoke bombs of the three-inch mortar burst upon the battery, and the columns of men rose like dragon's teeth from the rim of Blancmenil-le-bas wood to charge upon the enemy wire. Seven machine-gun posts wove their pattern of devastating fire over that narrowing field that was covered also by the bursts of many mortars.

There are moments when the song of man soars to a high note that the ear may not catch. That moment of the charge of Lovat's Commando was of that order.

Hampered in their dives by the F.W. 190's the R.A.F. cannon fighters had blasted the U.S. Rangers off their house tops with near misses and before they knew what had happened to them the two sergeants and Corporal Koons found themselves on the ground, but uninjured. Roused to a high pitch of inspiration by this event the Americans regained the roof to pour fire into the heart of the battery. The corporal was the first to recover.[1]

Meanwhile, as Lovat's Very lights had risen from the woodland to signal the attack the Commando fighter patrols breached the forward line of the enemy wire in two places with

[1] It is thought that Corporal F. Koons was the first U.S. soldier to kill a German in the Second World War.

Bangalores, and raced for the inner line. It seemed that no man could live in the race over that open space of death as the two troops came charging on, F Troop from the left and B Troop from the right. In the first split seconds Capt. R. G. Pettiward of the Beds and Herts Regiment and Lieut. J. A. Macdonald of the Royal Dragoons were killed as they rushed forward to lead F Troop across the open ground. But their deaths had given seconds to the living and Major Porteous, R.A., grasped the role of honour to lead the charge like a man possessed.

Within a minute the fleetest men of F Troop had gained and crossed the enemy first line of wire to dash on over the bodies of their dead and dying until they were upon the enemy. Even then, in those wild moments, the wounded were in the fight. Major Porteous, wounded three times, still held the lead as the enemy defence posts were overwhelmed at the bayonet point, and their guns silenced. C.S.M. Stockdale was seen to be firing from a sitting position, calmly picking off the enemy, and almost unaware that his left foot had been blown off.

B Troop to the right had fared better. The lie of the land had left them less exposed, and with fewer casualties they had blasted their way through the outer defences with grenades to sweep on like a storm to the very heart of the battery. There the German gunners died at the bayonet point beside their stricken guns. Only four enemy were found alive after the mad fury of that assault was spent. The rest had died or fled.

Even in their worst moments the Germans had not imagined a charge coming in against them with such startling suddenness over that open ground. They had stuck to their guns. But the assault had been a thing akin to madness, and out of which victory is sometimes fashioned.

The time was barely half past six o'clock when B Troop, using phosphorus and smoke, fell upon the last strong-points, enfilading the battery and threatening also the withdrawal of Major Mills Roberts and his men. The task was swiftly done. At ten minutes to seven o'clock, while B Troop took up all-round defensive positions, F Troop blew up the main group of five 15 cm. guns on the central emplacements. A few minutes later L/Cpl. Skerry, working single-handed, blew up the sixth gun on its lone site.

5

There was one last rite to be performed before No. 4 Commando quitted the sombre scene of their triumph. Swiftly the Commando had collected the bodies of eleven of their dead. These included the two officers killed as they had led the charge of F Troop from the cover of the wood. There was no time for a prolonged search. These eleven British dead were laid down upon the scorched and blackened earth of the gun site, and at a signal from Lord Lovat the Union Jack was run up over them while for a minute their comrades stood in silent salute. That was all.

Meanwhile three wounded officers and nineteen wounded men had been brought in, leaving thirteen others not accounted for and almost certainly dead. Already desultory German sniping urged the Commando to make all speed, and like shadows they moved off through the woods. But they did not withdraw by the way they had come. While the enemy watched and waited on the alert at Quiberville and the fast ebbing tide widened the dangerous gauntlet between the cliffs and the sea, Vasterival had still not engaged serious attention. In their careful planning No. 4 Commando had been fully alive to this possibility. While they had fought on shore their landing craft had withdrawn out to sea, and now, reinforced by three assault craft, they were coming in to Vasterival under the guns of the motor gun boat standing two miles offshore.

This was the last gamble, and on it the lives of the Commando must depend. In the withdrawal through the wood only the vicious snarl of rifle bullets warned that the enemy knew of their presence, and as the four German prisoners acting as stretcher bearers went down the gully trail blazed by C Troop to the beach, the first enemy shells were bursting some five hundred yards to the westward.

Every minute was vital, and the tide was ebbing fast as the wounded were floated out by men neck deep in the water to the landing craft. It was impossible for the craft to get in closer to the shore, but they had brought Goatley collapsible boats, and with these the wounded and many others were ferried across that still quiet stretch of shallow sea.

All went smoothly. As soon as each landing craft was filled it joined the motor gun boat while another immediately took its place. Smoke floats were launched to veil the last of those who waded out from Vasterival under growing enemy fire, and many men were seen at that time to aid their fellows. One trooper, stark naked but for a woollen cap comforter above his round red face, and a Mae West, ferried a collapsible boat with tremendous energy in the service of his comrades.

The re-embarkation had begun at half past seven o'clock, and within half an hour the last landing craft with the rearguard of No. 4 Commando turned seaward under cover of smoke, leaving Orange Beach One empty, even of the dead. There had not been a casualty in the withdrawal.

CHAPTER SEVEN

SEVEN O'CLOCK

THE news of the successful assault on the Orange Beaches and the final complete destruction of the Hess battery reached the Headquarters ship *Calpe* on time. It was almost the first clear and unmistakable news they had had since the five main columns of landing craft had set out upon their dangerous ventures. But in place of silence there was now a growing confusion of messages and reports, many of them suspect, all of them inconclusive.

Fifteen minutes before seven o'clock, while the Naval and Military Force Commanders had been deeply preoccupied with the problem of the Eastern headland, Bismarck, and with the imminent landing of the Fusiliers Mont-Royal to reinforce Red Beach, Commander Wyburd and Lt.-Colonel Durnford-Slater had arrived with their grim account of the disaster to Group 5 on the left flank. But even that message, undoubtedly authentic as far as it went, only made the more remarkable the failure of the Goebbels battery seriously to challenge the presence of so large a naval target off Dieppe.

But by that time there was much else to worry about. Whatever had happened on the Yellow Beaches was history: it could not be repaired: it was over. Here, impossible to observe through the almost continuous smoke-screens and the growing natural obscurity of the day, the fight was joined on the Dieppe beaches. The Royal Marine Commando was transhipping from the Chasseurs to landing craft ready for their new role, whatever it might be. That decision could not be long delayed, and there was little enough to go upon.

At precisely seven o'clock a message had reached the Headquarters ship asking for all landing craft to return to Blue Beach. Blue Beach had been a growing worry since the moment of the delayed getaway of the force. And now this was the first message, and it must be suspect.

What could it mean? The East headland was clearly and terribly under complete command of the Germans. The Rommel battery was still firing from behind Puits. Yet, if 'all landing craft' were needed urgently off Blue Beach the Royal Regiment of Canada must be there, anxious to re-embark and reasonably intact. What had happened on that beach in the two hours of silence?

If the Royal Regiment had held their own at Puits through that long period, why should they, a first-class regiment, wish to retire with all their tasks unfulfilled? The taking of the East headland had been a must in their orders. The Rommel battery had been an objective of the first importance.

The message added only to the doubts and fears. One thing alone was becoming very clear: the East headland, Bismarck, was the main key to Dieppe and to success.

But there was at this hour only a growing sense of unease in the minds of the Commanders striving to build up some kind of true picture from the meagre snippets of information coming in.

At four minutes past seven o'clock the Fusiliers Mont-Royal, emerging from the heavy smoke-screen laid by the destroyers, were about to land. Their success could resolve the problem of what best to do with the powerful Royal Marine Commando. Put in at the right time at the right place these men might crack the nut wide open.

Meanwhile the tide had taken a strong westerly set, and this, until then, unlooked-for factor had jeopardized the whole effectiveness of the landing of the Fusiliers Mont-Royal.

Only from Green Beach were the messages steady and re-assuring. The Queen's Own Cameron Highlanders, it seemed certain, had penetrated at least two and a half miles inland, and should by now have linked up with a squadron of tanks. The link had been planned for half past six o'clock. The South Saskatchewan Regiment were assaulting Quatre Vents Farm.

But Green Beach could not of itself have a decisive effect on the Dieppe beaches.

At twelve minutes past seven o'clock a message came in that the Casino building, a most important fortified strong-point on the West front of Dieppe, had fallen to the Royal Hamiltons. Twenty minutes later a further message stated that the sea wall had been breached in that area, and Brigadier Southam had ordered the tanks to go through. These messages, slight enough in themselves, were none the less heartening, and it seemed that White Beach was the one place where success might be exploited.

Nevertheless this must be very much a second best, and it was impossible to dismiss the possibilities of Blue Beach as a key to open the East headland. And then at twenty minutes to eight o'clock a message reached the *Calpe* that three companies of the Royal Regiment of Canada had landed successfully on Blue Beach. It added to similar messages 'out of the blue'. At best it merely recorded an event already more than two hours old.

Almost at the same time Air Marshal Leigh-Mallory at No. 11 Group Headquarters received a message purporting to come from the Military Force Commander cancelling further attacks against the Rommel battery and the East headland. He had picked up also the reassuring messages about Blue Beach. He was dubious in the extreme. One air attack was already on its way in against the Rommel battery and could not be diverted, as with misgivings Air Marshal Leigh-Mallory decided to act on the message.

The enemy by this time were beginning to warm up in the air, and their sorties had grown from an original thirty F.W. 190's to fifty fighter aircraft. This was not up to R.A.F. expectations, but there was still time. Enemy bombers were still absent.

The slow reaction of the Germans on land, sea and in the air, apart from the obvious strength of their coastal defences, was disconcerting. The naval reaction was nil. Tactical reconnaissance aircraft of the R.A.F., making many brave sorties inland and relying solely on their speed for safety, had failed to detect any troop movements in the area. It was in fact not until twenty-five minutes past seven o'clock that German G.H.Q. West showed any real awareness of the attacks:

The G.H.Q. West diary reads:

| 0725 hours | 10 Panzer Div. | Alarm Scale 11 |
| 0728 hours | S.S. Div. 'A.H.' | Alarm Scale 11 |

The enemy at that hour were feeling concern about reports from the neighbourhood of Pourville, Green Beach. They seemed unaware of a serious threat against Dieppe.

It was at this hour, and with this incomplete picture in his mind, that the Military Force Commander had to reach a decision to play his last card, the Royal Marine Commando. There were only three possible tasks: (i) the East headland, Red Beach;

(ii) the West headland, White Beach; (iii) Pourville, Green Beach.

It seemed to Major-General Roberts that Pourville was too far away for a decisive attack to be developed against the West headland, and a decisive attack he must have, otherwise it might be wiser to withhold the Royal Marines and send them safely home. Red Beach he had already reinforced, with what results he could not tell, and the feeling of a dangerous vacuum on Blue Beach added only to the mystery of the East headland.

Major-General Roberts came to the decision to reinforce White Beach. It seemed that there might be a chance that if this were done infantry might yet capture the West headland, and it would be possible then for the Engineers to carry out many demolitions before the hour of withdrawal.

The trickle of news coming in from White Beach gave by far the clearest picture. One thing was certain: it could never be right to reinforce weakness, and for Major-General Roberts to play his last card blind would have been nothing but a gambler's throw. The unmistakable odour of disaster had not begun to penetrate the fog of war, and it seemed possible—even probable—that success might be grasped.

To the east H.M.S. *Garth* was shelling the Eastern headland, and had turned her guns also upon cliff targets above Puits. She was, in fact, the only destroyer in touch with her Forward Observation Officer, Capt. C. A. Browne, R.C.A. Capt. Browne had established contact soon after five o'clock. He was somewhere behind the Eastern headland. He had landed on Blue Beach with the Royal Regiment of Canada.

Two assault landing craft had picked up the message purporting to come from Blue Beach, and asking for landing craft. They were on their way in.

CHAPTER EIGHT

BLUE BEACH

I

THE beach of Puits enclosed within the gentle-looking cliffs is a little more than two hundred yards from end to end. A sea wall of very solid masonry fills most of this expanse above high-water mark, and at normal tides there is about fifty yards of shingle bank between the wall and the water's edge. This shingle is of large rounded flints of from four to six inches in diameter. It is not an easy or a pleasant beach to walk on.

A footpath winds away up the cliffs from the north-east corner of the beach, and a lane leads straight up a narrow valley to the village of Puits. The lane in its valley is the principal landmark from seaward, but it is difficult to pick up at the best of times.

A few good houses overlook the small amphitheatre of the beach on both sides, and most outstanding, particularly in the half light of dawn, are some white houses on the crown of the cliffs to the east. It is a quiet sheltered place.

At low tide the beach extends to a depth of up to about three hundred yards. The shingle soon gives way to sand and flat rocks, and these rocks build up into rocky ledges which narrow the sea entrance to this small haven to less than one hundred and twenty yards. Even under good conditions the approach is not an easy exercise in navigation, and it is not difficult to miss Puits altogether in the ramifications of that coast.

Senior Landing Officer Lt.-Commander H. W. Goulding, D.S.O., R.N., leading the flotilla of landing craft of Group 3, carrying the Royal Regiment of Canada to their rendezvous at dawn on that morning of the 19th of August, knew well the nature of this beach and its difficulties. After the late start caused by the delay in forming up he had fixed his mind upon the problem of making up time. If he did not make up time he was well aware that the whole of this part of the expedition might prove abortive. Nevertheless, the Lt.-Commander could not take the risk of attempting to navigate direct for Puits. Instead he held to the

course which would give him a sight of the mile-wide gap of
Dieppe, and then altered course eastward to pick up the Blue
Beach valley.

That passage through the darkness of the early morning,
striving desperately to beat the dawn, was one of sustained and
menacing tension from which no man in all that convoy could
hope to be free. As the flotilla approached Dieppe the harbour
light flashed recognition signals, probably mistaking the dark
shapes of the flotilla for the convoy expected from the west—that
convoy that No. 4 Commando had so narrowly missed almost by
virtue of second sight.

The flashing light was disconcerting. It must have been obvious
to the watchers in Dieppe that this was not the convoy, and a
few minutes later a searchlight swept over the sea to discover the
landing craft and to hold them impaled with a feeling of helpless-
ness. Near the source of that streaming band of light, as soon as
they had destroyed it, they had an appointment with the Essex
Scottish Regiment, at this moment going in towards the Red
Beach of Dieppe. The searchlight was one of their minor objectives.

The flotilla held on its course, and for that last hour the
searchlight beam held them, revealing them to each other as
men whose faces had become like masks, and seeming to lay
them and their purpose bare and naked on the black swell of the
sea.

As the minutes dragged by the men in the landing craft
narrowed their minds to the awareness of a single deed. None
could know better the vital necessity of achieving surprise on the
narrow beach that lay ahead. Time alone had now rendered
surprise improbable in the extreme: they were too late, and only
a sleeping enemy could fail to see a flotilla of landing craft coming
in through the rock-lined channel to the small enclosure of that
beach of stones. The searchlight dispelled all possible illusion
of safety. Yet without hesitation, even with reckless speed, the
flotilla pressed on. They were, they knew, the key to open the
gates of Dieppe; perhaps the only key. Without them this whole
carefully planned raid might fail.

It is unlikely that the idea of turning back occurred to any of
them. They were committed. Lazily, relentlessly, the beam of
light seemed to draw the small ships along its broad shaft towards

the channel between the ledges of rock, and on to the grey and silent fringe of the auditorium of Puits.

As the flotilla came on through the channel the first enemy shots met them, single shots from the rifles of well-placed snipers, picking off men precisely, the men with signals apparatus, and others wearing badges of command. Major Schofield, and others in the first wave of landing craft, were dead or wounded before the beach was reached. But these few shots, idle and almost unhurried as they seemed, were but the tuning notes before the massive orchestra, grouped with its terrible instruments in all the recesses of the cliffs of Puits, answered the baton of command. As the first wave of landing craft touched down the whole skilful pattern of fire of the defences burst with appalling and devastating effect upon that band of men who came on like a sacrifice.

Heavy machine-guns, anti-tank guns, light A/A guns, mortars and even grenades greeted the arrival of the Royal Regiment of Canada on the Blue Beach of Puits seventeen minutes late, and from pill-boxes on the cliffs the enemy fired straight down into the wounded and shuddering flesh crowding the assault craft.

Yet in the face of almost certain death those officers who had thus far survived led their men with great shouts that died in their throats. And the men followed, climbing, clawing, over the bodies of their friends, struggling desperately to reach the sea wall across that narrow gauntlet of stones.

But from concrete pill-boxes embedded in the sea wall itself heavy machine-guns were firing point blank, themselves impregnable to small-arms fire, to mortar bombs, and even to the sustained covering fire from the guns of the motor gun boat standing in as near as she dared.

In those first seconds of landing men died in scores on the fringe of the sea, and it was clear that threads of a particular purpose were woven into that furious fire-pattern. These were the bullets of the snipers, unerringly picking off the officers and signallers. Most of the officers died at the moment of touch down, but in that death-trap the few who remained strove to lead onward to the wall. Even there most of them were pinned down by enfilade fire and forced into inaction. Yet men fired as they fell, and went on firing until they died of their wounds.

The sea wall at Puits is a solid piece of masonry rising vertically about ten or twelve feet above the shingle. The whole crest of the wall was crowned with wire, and the two flights of steps which break the front were filled with tangles of heavy barbed dannert wire. One of these flights of steps is at the west end of the wall, and the other near the middle.

All this had been well known to the attackers and carefully studied. It had been realized that on this beach above all timing was vital; that only a surprise assault might hope to sweep over this major obstacle before the defenders were fully on their toes.

The assault had been planned to come in in three waves with A and B Companies leading, followed by C and D Companies with the beach party to their right. The third wave, consisting of a special mortar detachment of the Black Watch of Canada, were to come in later.

In the event the second and third waves came in together. It was already 'later', so much later that this assault had become an act of sheer sacrificial defiance.

Faced by that shocking weight of fire C and D Companies somehow contrived to land at the extreme right of the beach under the cliffs beyond the western end of the sea wall. Here C Company in the most exposed position was at once caught by enfilade fire that held the men helpless and dying to the stones. Meanwhile D Company, with Lt.-Colonel Catto, the Commanding Officer, had got into a kind of re-entrant. The Company had suffered severely, but with a few men still behind him and able to move, the Colonel was resolved to cut a way through the wire in an attempt to gain the top of the cliffs and silence the guns that were mercilessly slaughtering his battalion from the houses. At that moment of dire urgency and need the loss of D Company's Bangalore torpedoes overboard, as they had transhipped into the landing craft in the absolute darkness of that early morning, was a calamity.

The official report compiled by Combined Operations Headquarters when all the facts were known of this landing reads:

'Notwithstanding that all the men followed their leaders promptly, an assault regiment on the offensive was transformed in minutes to less than two companies on the defensive. It was impossible to move. They lay watching for signs from their leaders.'

The signs from those few leaders who survived the landing were not wanting. Charging across that death-trap of stones with men of A and B Companies falling and following at his heels, Lt. W. G. R. Wedd reached the sea wall alone. Even in that moment when nothing but death seemed real Wedd had located the concrete pill-box on the sea wall from which the most devastating stream of direct fire was coming. His purpose was to silence that pill-box, and he silenced it. Seeming to gauge the speed of his own dying he stood straight up—for there was no other certain way—and hurled a grenade clean through the firing slit to kill every man within. His body was found there in front of the pill-box, testifying in the posture of death to the last act of living.

And Lt. Wedd was not alone. A few yards to his left Capt. C. G. Sinclair and Lt. L. C. Patterson had gained the wall unwounded. With the help of Corporal L. G. Ellis they had got their Bangalore torpedoes across the beach and within a yard or two of the central steps. There Patterson at once began to try to fix the Bangalores together determined to blow a gap in the wire. Unless that could be done there could be little hope for any of the men trapped on the narrow beach.

Meanwhile the mortar detachment of the Black Watch had landed, and with that same deliberation of purpose that had inspired Lt. Wedd, they managed to get off fifteen bombs against the white houses on the cliffs to the left. There was no time for more before they died to the last man, but they had achieved in that flurry of attack some cover for Lt. Patterson, striving now desperately to get the Bangalore torpedoes into action, but the locking device had become jammed with stones.

Hurricane bombers were now attacking the cliff defences with smoke, but a rising wind was helping the enemy. Meanwhile on the beach Lt. Patterson was brought down suffering many wounds, and with his clothing in flames at the very moment of freeing the jammed torpedoes.

While those men near enough tried to smother the burning clothing of the dying man, Capt. Sinclair took over the Bangalore torpedoes and at last succeeded in getting them into position. It was too late. Pinned down, seeking the shelter of the dead, the remnants of a regiment were selling their lives, firing steadily with their rifles and their few Bren guns, to challenge the defences until the end. From the sea two of the landing craft were giving all the covering fire they could bring to bear, disdaining the possible safety of the sea beyond the channel. For them also there could be but one end.

Capt. Sinclair with Corporal Ellis under the sea wall, sheltered in the concentration of their effort to blow the wire, were almost unaware of the tragedy that fast enclosed them, and at last Sinclair blew a gap in the wire. Without a moment's hesitation Corporal Ellis wriggled his way through, and gained the shelter of some bushes to the west of the gully behind the beach. He was unharmed. There he lay for a while getting his bearings, and watching the gap in the wire through which he had crawled. No one came. Then the Corporal made his way inland to do what he could single-handed with his rifle against the enemy. He was the only man out of three companies to get off the Blue Beach of Puits.

Over on the extreme right three officers, a sergeant and eleven men, mostly of D Company, were still behind their Colonel using the best of the doubtful cover on all that dreadful place of death. Undismayed by the loss of the Bangalore torpedoes, the Colonel, with Sergeant Coles at his side, had attacked the massive tangle of wire with wire cutters and the two of them, covered by Lt. Stewart with the Bren gun for more than forty minutes, had carved a way through. At the last Lt. Stewart had risen to his feet, firing from the hip with the Bren to defend his Colonel against increasing enemy pressure. In that defiant pose Stewart survived for two or three minutes until the Colonel and Sergeant were through the wire followed by Capt. Browne, the Forward Observation Officer of the destroyer *Garth*, and the eleven men.

These few, with Corporal Ellis, were the only men out of a regiment to get off Blue Beach. The time was then ten minutes past six o'clock. The fire of A and B Companies had dwindled almost to nothing. All that remained of C and D Companies were in the re-entrant at the junction of the sea wall where they had landed. They could not locate the machine-gun positions enfilading them from both flanks. They lay powerless and trapped.

And now the German mortars, ranging with uncanny accuracy, were dropping their bombs almost under the wall, seeking out the survivors from their meagre shelter, while the elated Germans on the cliffs hurled down grenades in triumph.

2

Once through the wire Lt.-Colonel Catto led his small band of men swiftly to the cliff top. There were no further obstacles, and their sudden appearance seems to have unnerved the enemy. They rushed the first of the fortified houses, overwhelming the small garrison at their guns, and then moving on from house to house. To their surprise all the remaining houses were deserted, abandoned almost in panic by the enemy.

This unexpected assault had markedly reduced the enemy fire from the right flank, and at seven o'clock, having accomplished all that seemed possible in that quarter, the Colonel tried to lead his men back by the way they had come, hoping that even now it might not be too late to rally a few more survivors to make a last bid. But the gap in the wire had been quickly detected and covered by heavy enemy fire. The line of retreat was closed. At the same time a strong enemy patrol was seen moving up against the Colonel and his men from the left. About a hundred yards westward there was some slight cover. It was the only possible way out, and the Colonel led on, crouching at the double, under the cover of a low wall. For the moment they were safe.

Meanwhile Corporal Ellis on his lonely mission had entered one or two houses on the outskirts of Puits, sniping the enemy and engaging a machine-gun post with his rifle. There was not much more that he could do alone, and at last he began to make his way back to the beach. It was almost at the exact moment when the Colonel was eluding the enemy patrol. Without difficulty the Corporal reached the sea wall and managed to crawl back through the gap in the wire blown by Capt. Sinclair.

It was not until he reached the beach that Ellis began to realize the disaster that had overwhelmed his regiment. The shattering impact of the enemy fire at the moment of landing had disintegrated the companies, platoons, sections, leaving men alone, absorbed in the tasks or struggles of their narrowing worlds. There was almost no firing from the beach, and it was some time, as he crouched there, before Ellis could make out the living from the dead in all that grotesque tangle of sprawling bodies. The two landing craft that had given support fire in the early stages had limped away, their guns silenced, their gunners dead. It was nearing half past seven o'clock. The tide was ebbing fast, lengthening the gauntlet of stones to the wet sand and the flat rocks.

There were moments even of intense silence, creating the illusion that it was a place only of the dead. Yet the cliffs, the pill-boxes, all the defensive posts of the enemy were manned by living men searching that bloodstained shambles for movement.

It seemed to those who still lived, and there were then upwards of one hundred still alive, that their plight must be known. They lay still, searching the narrow channel of the sea from which help must come.

From the moment of landing until twenty-three minutes to eight o'clock that morning, Capt. Browne, lying up with Lt.-Colonel Catto's party, had contrived to keep some contact with his destroyer. His position made his observations of little value, but he had called urgently and constantly for fire to be brought down upon the houses on the cliffs. At twenty minutes to eight, at the same moment as a squadron of Hurricane fighter-bombers attacked the East headland, the *Garth* opened fire. And it was in the midst of that diversion that the two assault landing craft which had picked up the urgent call from Blue Beach—almost surely an enemy message—sailed bravely through the narrow channel. They came in steadily.

It is possible that few men surviving on that beach had much idea of anything beyond themselves, or were even aware that others were living. As the leading assault craft came in to the shallows with her doors open and her ramp down, men rose from the huddled heaps of the dead to rush out over the hard wet sand, and to overwhelm her with their weight of numbers. Until that moment the enemy had held his fire. With men clinging to every finger-hold, the craft filling rapidly with water, her doors jammed open and her ramp down, the assault craft was a sitting duck. Slowly, under terrific bursts of concentrated fire, she tried to back away, her ramp dragging like a smashed limb. She was fifty yards out when a direct hit from a shell capsized her. Then for a few minutes there was a wild flurry in the sea, as from the last struggles of some great harpooned fish, as the bullets of enemy machine-guns and snipers whipped the waters amidst the tumult of struggling men. Only one man survived to be picked up at sea four hours later.

The second landing craft fared much better. In the attempt to reach her many men died in the torrent of machine-gun fire that spewed over all the foreshore, but in their dying they enabled a few to get away safely.

This was the first of many attempts that morning. Hour after hour, while it was thought that there might still be life, the crews of the landing craft strove to close Blue Beach in the face of a murderous fire relieved of all other defensive tasks.

In the end, out of 27 officers and 516 men of the Royal Regiment of Canada, 3 officers and 57 men returned. Many others, men of the Black Watch of Canada, of the Royal Canadian Artillery, and of the landing craft, died on Blue Beach and on the fringe of the sea.

CHAPTER NINE

EIGHT O'CLOCK

AT EIGHT o'clock German General Headquarters West recorded the first attempts of the British to gain a bridgehead at Dieppe. Twenty-five minutes later the highest state of readiness was ordered, and the 10th Panzer Division and the A.H. SS Division were poised ready to move. But it was the reports from Pourville, Green Beach, that were causing the enemy the greatest uneasiness.

The almost continuous smoke-screens laid by aircraft, destroyers, gun boats and landing craft added to the smoke and flame of bombing and battle and the deteriorating weather conditions swathed all the coast and seaway in front of Dieppe in a growing obscurity. In that dark sea forest of small ships, landing craft, gun boats, motor launches and destroyers bustled incessantly about their business, answering calls for close support of the main beaches, rescuing men from the sea, ferrying wounded, taking disabled craft in tow, and evading as best they could the enemy bombardment directed against them. The naval crews, especially of the landing craft, were suffering heavy casualties.

Towards the outer seaward fringes of the smoke, in the midst of a growing hubbub of small vessels, many of them seeking aid and to disembark wounded, Lt.-Commander J. H. Wallace, R.N., handled H.M.S. *Calpe* with a sustained brilliance duly praised in the official records. The business of *Calpe* was not only that of parent ship of all this brood, the heart and head of all the comings and goings, but also she was in the fight, bringing her guns to bear wherever they might be needed most, while her A/A gunners defended her against the growing threat from the skies.

On the bridge of the destroyer by the side of Lt.-Commander Wallace, Air Commodore Cole maintained a ceaseless vigil of the skies and kept close contact with his Headquarters at No. 11 Group Fighter Command. Other observers, including Commander E. N. Strauss of the U.S. Navy, strove to follow the developing pattern of the combined land, sea and air operation. The trend of events on shore remained almost totally obscure. More than 5,000 men had been committed on the beaches together with a probable thirty Churchill Infantry tanks of the first flight. Three hours had passed since zero. The land battle must be lost or won. They did not know.

Working with his Staff Officers in the Operations room of the Headquarters ship the Military Force Commander grasped each tiny fragment of information, evaluating, checking, balancing message against message, listening to the verbal reports of seamen of the landing craft, and the painful and disjointed remarks of wounded men. But the picture was not forming clearly. It was like a jig-saw puzzle with small clusters of pieces fitting together in jagged patterns here and there, yet giving little or no clue to the main design.

On the right flank the puzzle was building up with some promise, and it was from Pourville, Green Beach, that the most continuous and coherent stream of messages had been maintained. Then at seventeen minutes past eight o'clock a report reached *Calpe* that White Beach was under control, and that the tanks were making progress. If that were true some of the blank spaces on the right should soon be filled. The last preparations of the Royal Marine Commando were completed under the direction of Commander Ryder. The news looked good for them. They were ready to go in.

Yet it was evident that the success of the landings at Green Beach, Pourville, were not being exploited with sufficient speed. The landings on the inner flanks at Puits and Pourville should have tied in with the main assault on the Red and White Beaches not later than half past six o'clock in the performance of many common tasks. The Royal Regiment of Canada, swinging right-handed from Puits, should have joined with elements of the Essex Scottish Regiment moving round the flank of the East headland from Red Beach. The Rommel battery, whose shells were one of the major harassments of this hour at sea, should have been silenced. Royal Canadian Engineers, supported by the Royal Regiment, should have blown the Gas Works. A score of light A/A guns, bristling in the area, and spouting their shells into the clouding sky, gave constant proof that the Royal Regiment and the Essex Scottish had failed to destroy them.

It was natural in these circumstances that interest and the weight of endeavour must shift to the right flank. There also there were grave omissions. The tanks of the Calgary Regiment should have joined the Queen's Own Cameron Highlanders of Canada in the attacks planned to develop against the aerodrome at St. Aubin and the Headquarters of the German 110 Division, believed to be in the château of Arques la Bataille. That rendezvous with the tanks was timed for half past six o'clock. At best, in view of the last message from White Beach, they would be two hours late.

There was more hope in the possibilities of the Royal Hamilton Light Infantry. It had been planned for them to go in against Quatre Vents Farm from the East to support the South Saskatchewan Regiment in their frontal assault on this powerful fortified position. Without them it was doubtful whether the South Saskatchewan Regiment could succeed. Finally the West headland itself should be gravely threatened. And there were some signs in all this tangle of fragments that this might be so.

The right flank was the place of hope.

Nor had hope been abandoned elsewhere. The blowing of the lock gates and gear and the destruction of the Floating Dock in the Bassin de Paris might yet be accomplished along with many other demolition tasks.

Following on the heels of the reassuring news from White Beach, Lt.-Commander Goulding reported personally on board *Calpe* that he had landed the Royal Regiment of Canada on the Blue Beach of Puits. He did not give the impression that the landing was unsuccessful. This was baffling news, but the Military Force Commander acted on it to the extent of countermanding orders for more bombing attacks against the Rommel battery and the East headland. There must be just a chance that the Royal Regiment, frustrated in their main tasks, might yet succeed in others. At least one emergency air-landing strip should be established in the rear of the East headland, or on the racecourse.

The sands of time were running out fast. The withdrawal had been planned to occupy three and a half hours. Long before then enemy reinforcements would be reaching the whole area in some strength. Horse-drawn heavy mortars, used as howitzers, were already adding appreciably to the weight of fire coming down on Red, White and Green Beaches. Soon Divisional and Corps artillery must be expected to supplement the fixed defences of the coast.

Wounded men were now being transhipped to the *Calpe* and *Fernie* by a constant stream of landing craft ferrying from the main beaches. There were more than two hundred wounded on board *Calpe*, not including one quarter of her own crew. These numbers were not, however, in excess of expectations.

It was in this hour between eight and nine o'clock that a report of the first attempt at German naval interference reached the Naval Force Commander. Ten German E-boats from Boulogne were reported approaching from the North-East, and *Slazak*, *Brocklesby* and *Bleasdale* were sent to intercept. This greatly diminished the sad lack of fire-power that could be brought to bear against the headlands and in support of the men ashore. In the event the message proved false.

There were as yet no enemy bombers overhead, but the naval gunners were warming to their task as the fighters dived out of the clouds to harass the multitude of vessels with machine-gun fire. At this time the German Air Force in the West was tardily becoming aware of the challenge, and preparing to accept it.

Meanwhile Lt.-Commander Goulding, joined by Lt.-Commander McMullen, boarded two motor launches to return to Blue Beach with all the landing craft they could muster. Whatever had happened, the hour of withdrawal was fast approaching, and definite news must be gained. The continued activity of the enemy in all that quarter enhanced the silence of the Royal Regiment.

As the minutes ticked by with a sense of increasing gravity the whole position of Green Beach began to assume a major importance in the minds of the Naval and Military Force Commanders. Lt.-Commander Prior, who had led in the South Saskatchewan Regiment to land, and had then received the Queen's Own Cameron Highlanders of Canada on the beach itself, had given a full and coherent account of progress as far as he knew it. That they had gone ashore and made progress inland was beyond a doubt.

At this stage Commander McClintock, R.N., was standing by for orders. These were not yet formulated in the minds of the Commanders. A great deal depended on the success of the Royal Marines. The next hour would tell. It must be the crucial hour. It was then half past eight o'clock.

CHAPTER TEN

GREEN BEACH

I

IN THE last moment of the dawn twilight A Company of the South Saskatchewan Regiment dashed from their assault craft on the shingle fringe of Pourville beach and on over the heavy stones to gain the cliffs. They had won their moment of immunity, and as the ring of boots on shingle roused the enemy to action A Company was already scaling the steep cliffs with their tubular steel ladders.

They had touched down at five minutes to five o'clock, five minutes late, but still within the narrow margin which could mean success or failure.

Following the explosion of the grenade, which had wounded seventeen of their number on the passage in H.M.S. *Invicta*, the whole operation had gone smoothly. Such an accident could be taken by the men as an omen for good or ill. Fortunately it had served to inspire rather than to dispirit. This had been their hard luck. The regiment had transhipped to assault craft from *Beatrix* and *Invicta* with faultless precision and speed. Their escorts, the Motor Gun Boat 317 and two medium support landing craft, were ready to lead them in with Lt.-Commander R. M. Prior in command.

And from that first moment the rhythm had held, bringing them in to land at the peak of their readiness. There were no difficult navigational problems. The dark gash of Dieppe between its headlands yawned on the port bow of the leading vessel, and the ravine of the River Scie, breaking the line of the Pourville cliffs with its dark shadow, was easily seen. They had slid quietly in to land on that eight hundred yards wide stony beach before the enemy awoke to the challenge.

But there was no immunity for the second wave. Already as C Company reached the beach the enemy mortars and machine-guns came into action, shattering the twilight with their deadly fire, and blasting the flint shingle in all the angles of the groynes that spaced the beach at intervals of one hundred yards.

Nevertheless the South Saskatchewan Regiment had caught the enemy off balance, uncertain of his targets in the difficult light, and uneasy that some of the invaders had eluded his guns. Nine-tenths of that opening outburst of fire was on fixed lines, and the Company Commanders quickly realized it, holding their men to the open spaces away from the groynes. Cover was more dangerous than open ground, and in those minutes of enemy uncertainty the three companies of the regiment rushed at the heels of their officers over that dangerous tract. To pause would have been fatal not only to themselves. Upon the speed of their own attack the safety of the Queen's Own Cameron Highlanders of Canada must depend, and they knew it.

The Camerons were due to land at an interval of thirty minutes, and only the success of the South Sasks in these opening stages could lessen the weight of fire that the Camerons would be called upon to bear.

Swiftly scaling the cliffs A Company captured two pill-boxes, and lost half a dozen men in a third that blew up at a touch. It was not the only booby trap on those heavily fortified cliffs, laced with trip wires and guarding 'La Maison Blanche', the Head-quarters Officers' Mess of the German Coastal Defence in the area. But most of the booby traps showed a remarkable naivety of imagination. Here and there tins of pineapple were lying about, but these were so out of place in this setting as to be instantly suspect. In any case A Company had not much time for tinned pineapple as they swung left-handed to attack a light A/A battery of three guns that was already shelling the landing craft from the rear of the West headland.[1] A Company rushed the battery and took it at the point of the bayonet before the gunners were aware that the invaders were off the beach. The Company then moved on towards their principal objective, the Radar Station behind the West headland.

It seemed at first that their momentum must carry them through to victory, but at once beyond the battery position they ran into a patch of swamp, and were almost trapped before they could find a way round. Twenty minutes of probing finally extricated them, spurred on by the sounds of battle in Pourville itself.

[1] The Dieppe West headland, 'Hindenburg', flanking the East of Pourville beach.

C Company moving fast off the beach had rushed the village of Pourville to meet a strong force of enemy head on in the main street. The skirmish was short and sharp. Within twenty minutes there were fifteen enemy dead in the road, and the South Sasks had possession of Pourville and opened up the way through. A second platoon of C Company, having dispersed a strong enemy patrol near a group of sheds on the outskirts of the village, were facing and holding a strong counter attack. By that time A Company had run into a road block which they were striving to outflank under heavy mortar fire in order to come to grips with the defences of the Radar Station.

It was clear that this whole area was strongly defended by skilfully placed pill-boxes and strong-points, mobile patrols, and well-thought-out patterns of cross-fire from heavy machine-guns and mortars coming down on road junctions, bridges and other key points. The snipers, too, held their ground and waited for troops to pass before picking off their prey.

In a sheltered position near the cliff top stood La Maison Blanche. Within a mile to the South of Pourville village was the heavily defended position of Quatre Vents Farm covering the approaches to St. Aubin aerodrome and the south-west flank of the château of Arques la Bataille.

Lt.-Colonel Merritt, the Commanding Officer of the South Saskatchewan Regiment, knew that his hopes of success lay in speed and a quick link-up with the Royal Hamilton Light Infantry in the attack against Quatre Vents Farm. Leaving Pourville to C Company the Colonel led B and D Companies through the houses of the village while C Company was still fighting in the main street and on the flanks. No doubt this move had an un-nerving effect on the enemy fighting in the village.

Without delay B and D Companies gained the road beyond and pressed on to a bridge across the River Scie. Once across that bridge the South Sasks would be in a position to attack Quatre Vents Farm before such an attack was expected by the enemy.

The role of A and C Companies was to gain Pourville and the rear of the (Dieppe) West headland threatening Pourville beach, and secure the line of withdrawal. They were also to attack and capture La Maison Blanche and eliminate pill-boxes and all possible machine-gun posts. Unless these two companies were successful the bulk of the South Saskatchewan Regiment and the whole of the Queen's Own Cameron Highlanders of Canada would be trapped.

Immediately after crossing the beach one platoon of C Company had moved right-handed along the edge of the cliffs, opening fire on La Maison Blanche, and at once the platoon came under heavy fire from enemy positions in the ravine and from snipers. It was a position of the utmost danger, calling for determined action, and Lt. L. R. McIlveen, leading his platoon, was equal to it. To be forced on to the defensive was to fail, probably to die. Without faltering for an instant McIlveen charged for La Maison Blanche, over-running the enemy positions and smothering their fire before they had a clear sight of him and his men. Within ten minutes the enemy fortified building had fallen, its defenders killed, its communications smashed. With that bold stroke the platoon had captured an objective of great importance, but their position was far from secure. Enemy defence posts in the rear as well as the enemy in the ravine began at once to harass the new garrison. French girls, appearing from the cellars where they had hidden at the first onslaught, joined with McIlveen's men helping to barricade windows with mattresses, and through all that morning these girls served wine and cakes to the troops manning the firing positions.

Meanwhile McIlveen had driven the enemy out of the ravine with a barrage from a captured three-inch mortar, and had sent a section to attack a machine-gun post to the West that was enfilading the Camerons as they came in to land.

2

The success of the landing of the South Saskatchewan Regiment, and the speed with which they had gone in to the attack, had done a great deal to lessen the weight of fire the enemy were able to bring to bear, but the mortars covering the groynes with predicted fire were fanning the shingle with a hail of fragments of flint and steel.

From the outset the guns of the Motor Gun Boat 317 had been firing with great accuracy and had scored direct hits against machine-gun positions, but the prospect of the beach demanded qualities of the highest courage in those who would land upon it.

At ten minutes past five o'clock, having seen the South Saskatchewan Regiment safely off the beach, Lt.-Commander Prior ordered a support landing craft to put him ashore with a small beach party to receive the Camerons. At that time the enemy had recovered from the first surprise and was concentrating all his fire-power on the fringe of the sea in an endeavour to prevent further landings. An A/A shell hit Prior's landing craft fifty yards out, but he at once got aboard another and went on in with the motor gun boat and two support craft blazing away with everything they could bring to bear.

Less than a mile out to sea the Camerons were then clearly seen coming in. They had sailed from Newhaven in twenty-five personnel landing craft and had kept their stations steadily all through the night. For them perhaps, of all those men landing on the beaches on that day, it might have been better to be late than early. They were on time within ten minutes. One thousand yards offshore Lt.-Colonel Gostling gave the order 'Prepare to Land'. It was a stirring order. They could see the land ahead, the broad enclosure of the shingle beach swirling with the smoke and flame of gunfire. In these Canadians of the Queen's Own Cameron Highlanders there was no place for that tension of speculation of to be or not to be: that *plage* of shattered stones might be their *abattoir*.

On the command 'Prepare to Land' a piper stood at once unbidden like a figurehead in the leading craft, and the strange wild music of war and the misty silent hills swelled out across the water, a dirge and a challenge, lifting men's hearts to their throats, and wrapping itself in mysterious fashion round the entrails of the enemy. On the lament of that brave music of the pipes the landing craft bearing the Camerons came steadily on.

Lt.-Commander Prior and his beach group heard that music, and so also did McIlveen's men behind their barricades in La Maison Blanche—so also did many Germans in their machine-gun posts.

Over all that one thousand yards of lonely sea the piper piped 'The Hundred Pipers'. It was in the ears of Lt.-Colonel Gostling and many others as they died at the touchdown, but the music did not die. It seemed to carry Major Law, as he took command, and the Camerons, in a great charge across the beach to gain the cliffs of Pourville, as though borne on the wild surge of the pipes.

It was the task of the Camerons to press on through to the outskirts of St. Aubin aerodrome. On the edge of a little wood, the Bois de Vertus, they had a rendezvous with the tanks of the Calgary Regiment. With the tanks they would attack the aerodrome, and then turn north-east against the château of Arques la Bataille. A brief conference with Battalion rear Headquarters of the South Saskatchewan Regiment in Pourville gave Major Law a sketchy picture. Well-sited pill-boxes, deadly mortar fire outranging our own mortars by as much as six or seven hundred yards, and daring sniping, were holding up B and D Companies at the bridge crossing of the Scie. As yet the power of Quatre Vents Farm had not been weakened.

Because of that Major Law led the Camerons along the West bank of the Scie, and detached part of one company to attack some pill-boxes holding up the South Sasks. It was by then six o'clock. The South Sasks were more than holding their own in the area of Pourville itself. The Camerons were moving through to the South-West to Bas de Hautot, coming under heavy mortar fire from Quatre Vents Farm as they attempted to storm a bridge across the Scie that would open up the road to the Bois de Vertus. The whole operation was on time.

3

As soon as Lt.-Colonel Merritt had cleared Pourville with B and D Companies, heavy mortar and machine-gun fire had come down at the point of the river crossing. All the way along the road snipers had held their fire until the men had passed, and as the leading platoon reached the bridge there was a moment of crisis calling for the highest qualities of leadership. As men took to the water Lt.-Colonel Merritt walked calmly across the bridge waving his tin helmet round his head, and calling: "See, there is no danger here!"

As though he strolled in St. James's Park of a Summer morning he led four parties of men across the bridge in the face of a barrage, and then led his two companies into the attack.

From the outset it was a position of great gravity. The line of retreat was covered by deadly fire, and the snipers picked off the battalion runners trying to maintain contact with Pourville.

Finally, the Colonel acted as his own runner, and also organized a series of attacks against the pill-boxes defending the perimeter of Quatre Vents Farm.

Time after time these attacks were driven back, and after more than an hour of bitter fighting little or no impression had been made on the enemy. Without artillery support, and without the promised attack from the East by the Royal Hamilton Light Infantry, it looked as if B and D Companies would be lucky to hold their own, and maintain some pressure against the Farm. This much was vital in order to hold open the line of retreat for the Camerons.

It was soon after seven o'clock when Private O. O. Fenner leapt from cover to charge the main enemy position firing his Bren gun from the hip. At once Major McTavish rushed into the attack with B and D Companies in full cry, to carry the outer defences in the wake of that sudden act of bravery.

For yet another hour the two companies fought with dogged determination, outgunned by the enemy, and ceaselessly harassed by mortar fire, while the defenders of Quatre Vents Farm hung on grimly. It was a stalemate. Long before nine o'clock Lt.-Colonel Merritt had realized that the Royal Hamilton Light Infantry would not be there. He could not take the Farm, but he could hang on to hold open the line of retreat for the Camerons.

Meanwhile A Company, using their smoke canisters, had at last found a way round the road block that had held them up. For a time they had taken cover in a shallow ravine, and from that point had tried to organize an attack against the Radar Station. They had then reached a position two hundred yards from their goal, but without artillery support the enemy frustrated all their efforts to break through.

At one stage, Private Sawden charging a pill-box single-handed had killed six Germans and silenced the gun, but the Radar Station was too well secured to yield to individual acts of heroism. A Company needed fire-power, and they had not enough. But they were not without hope. Capt. H. B. Carswell, the Forward Observation Officer of the destroyer *Albrighton*, had landed with them and had made contact with his ship. As a result by half past six o'clock the guns of *Albrighton* were destroying machine-gun posts and A/A batteries on the Western headland, and adding greatly to the chances of both battalions in their final withdrawal.

At fifteen minutes to nine o'clock the Camerons had reached a point two and a half miles inland and were still seeking the tanks that had been due to meet them at half past six o'clock. It was already clear to the Camerons that they would have to fight their way out, and that every minute made their position more dangerous. They had had several stiff skirmishes with enemy patrols, and at the outset they had come under heavy mortar fire in trying to force a crossing of the Scie. Finally they had abandoned that idea, and had pressed on in a detour, moving fast and well to the edge of Bernonville wood. They had then crossed open country, casting round for signs of support in all the area of Bois de Vertus.

Then, as the time filtered away to the planned hour of withdrawal, the Camerons prepared for their return journey through that dangerous country. They could only hope that the South Saskatchewan Regiment had managed to hold open the door. At ten o'clock the landing craft were due to come in again to Green Beach, and the steel band of enemy pressure was fast tightening round the area, striving to compress all these men into the narrow enclosure of the beach and kill them.

Through all that time Lt.-Commander Prior had lived and worked on the beach, seeming unaware of danger, and with the help of Lt. R. D. Miller some shelter had been found for the worst of the wounded. Capt. F. W. Hayter, the medical officer, had somehow established three Regimental Aid Posts, and under incessant fire these three men worked with quiet and sustained gallantry.

The position was deteriorating steadily.

Time after time Lt.-Commander Prior had tried to signal the motor gun boat for fire to be brought down upon hill positions that were especially threatening, but without result. The gun boat was doing all she could, but she had failed to land her Beachmaster and the beach signal party. Despite the well-directed fire of the *Albrighton* the beach was still under heavy mortar and machine-gun fire and well covered by snipers.

At nine o'clock an assault landing craft attempted to close the beach, but was driven off. The tide was ebbing fast, widening that deadly strip over which two battalions of men must pass. It was a desperate prospect.

CHAPTER ELEVEN

THE MAIN ASSAULT

I

THE growing thunder of war closing in upon them from the flanks before the dawn had aroused the people of Dieppe from sleep with a sense of excitement, compounded of hope as well as of fear. They were accustomed in these years of the Nazi occupation of their land to the alarms and dangers of air raids. They had listened often, and without comfort, to the harsh roar of anti-aircraft fire and the crump of bombs, but this rousing din of war was of a different texture and pattern.

On all that broad sea front of Dieppe the Germans, too, had awakened to a new alertness. In the grey light of dawn they could see little beyond the fringe of the sea, but the sense of some crisis impending was unescapable, as battles raged on the flanking beaches.

Along the whole length of the foreshore from the end of the West jetty breakwater to the steep white cliffs of the Western headland, the heavy barbed coils of triple dannert wire grew out of the half light, seeming a fragile barrier, little more than a snare for the unwary in its almost delicate filigree of outline. Fifteen feet behind the rolls of dannert a seven foot wire apron fence built on the knife-rest principle gave a more solid impression to the watchers at their posts behind the sea wall, on the house tops, in the pill-boxes and casemates, behind the anti-tank blocks and barricades, and in the caves of the headlands. Even then, as they stared outwards to the quiet sea, they looked also over their shoulders, for the threat—if threat there was—might come equally well round the flanks of the headlands from Pourville and Puits.

The beach of Dieppe is a steep shingle bank rising from about 1 in 40 gradient to 1 in 10 under the solid masonry and concrete of the sea wall. In places the high tides had piled up the shingle almost to the top of the wall, which normally rose vertically ten feet above the beach. But this might prove more of a hindrance than a help to an enemy seeking a foothold. The sea wall, protecting the wide promenade, filled all the front for fifteen hundred yards from the harbour to the West headland. It was well fortified. At regular intervals along its whole length men peered out from under cowlings such as shield 'prompters' on a stage. These men were Forward Observation Officers. Their stage was the wide beach, and those they must prompt were far behind them manning the batteries of mortars and field-guns that could bring down concentrations of fire anywhere upon all that steep and stony foreshore at a word. This was in addition to the predicted fire of mortars that would fall upon the angles of the wooden groynes which run up out of the sea to space the beach into tracts one hundred and fifty yards wide. There were, in fact, a wealth of weapons in great variety concentrated upon this shore.

The Germans, when their own invasion hopes had dwindled, had worked with an energy and skill born of a growing fear throughout all the Summer in their preparations to meet an invader. There had been much talk and clamour for an invasion, and the Germans had constructed skilfully an 'iron coast' to meet it when it should come. They had burrowed tunnels and dug crawl trenches to their 'prompters' boxes' and grenade pits from the hotels and boarding houses that stood in gaunt and sombre outline in the half dark beyond the wide boulevards Marechal Foch and Verdun. These boulevards were wide enough to take three lines of traffic, and between them lay lawns and gardens, a peaceful seeming expanse twelve hundred yards long by more than one hundred and fifty feet wide, and lending a spaciousness to the front of the huddled seaport town. The line of those tall buildings seemed like a wedge, imprisoning the rambling town and holding open the mouth of the narrow valley of the D'Arques that encloses Dieppe within the limits of its white chalk hills.

To the casual eye there were few signs of life at five o'clock on the morning of the 19th August. In all that sober row of hotels and boarding houses looking bleakly out over the grey sea, no guest lay waking or sleeping, and no light burned. The white mass of the Casino building with its forecourt and steps breaking the line of the sea wall at the western end of the promenade had a blank deserted look, as though long abandoned. It had long since ceased to be a place of gambling and amusement, and had become instead a minor fortress. In the white cliffs of the headlands there was no sign of weapons or of movement in the blank sockets of the caves. In the docks of the inner harbour armed trawlers and invasion barges lay dark and silent at their berths, while the incessant bursts of gunfire flickered staccato patterns in the sky above the headlands, and beyond to the east and west.

At that hour of five o'clock in the morning the sea in front of Dieppe appeared as deserted as Dieppe itself, revealing nothing to the eyes of the watchers. Even from the snipers high up on the roofs of many buildings the last of the dawn twilight hid its secret.

Three miles offshore at that hour a great concourse of little ships, deployed in a wide arc and carrying the men of the main assault, bore steadily in at 10 knots to close the beaches at the appointed hour. They hoped simply to come in tight on the heels of a brief bombardment from the air and sea. Greater surprise than this they could not hope to gain.

The motor gun boat of Lt.-Commander Mullen was in the lead. Gun boats and motor launches, flak and support landing craft guarded the heart and flanks and rear of the convoy ready to give close support with their machine-guns and Oerlikons.

On the left sailed the assault landing craft with the Essex Scottish Regiment under Lt.-Colonel F. K. Jasperson, bound for the Red Beach, east. On the right were the assault landing craft of the Royal Hamilton Light Infantry under Lt.-Colonel R. R. Labatt, bound for the White Beach, west.

And in their midst with the flak and support craft, and in the van of those who must be first to land, were the Beach Assault Group of nearly four hundred sappers of the Royal Canadian Engineers with their special roles of blasting the sea wall, and all else that might stand in the way of men and tanks.

Keeping station close in along the line in the second rank loomed the larger shapes of the tank landing craft of the first wave. Behind them again came the landing craft with the mortar detachments of the Black Watch of Canada and the Calgary Highlanders, and the machine-gunners of the Toronto Scottish.

Bravely they came on with all the expanse of Dieppe and its beaches in their minds' eyes, knowing well the slope of the shingle, widening in an arc from left to right from a depth of 180 yards in the east, the Red Beach of the Essex Scottish, to 360 yards in the west, the White Beach where the Royal Hamilton Light Infantry must land. Much they knew; much more they imagined.

Above all they knew that they must seize the beaches at one bound, and press on to their tasks. So they waited like runners poised for the starter's pistol, ready to dash for the sea wall.

In the rear and on the eastern flank of the convoy six assault craft altered course eastward as they made the landfall of the Dieppe Gap. These were the assault craft of the Infantry Landing Ship *Duke of Wellington*, carrying the mortar detachment of the Black Watch for their appointment with death on the Blue Beach of Puits. The main body of ships held on its course dead ahead. The moment of revelation was at hand.

Out of the Northern sky the low hum of aircraft grew to a roar as Bostons and Blenheims swooped in upon the East headland pouring out a dense curtain of smoke, while Hurricane cannon fighters, fighter-bombers and Spitfires dived in a fierce blaze of guns and hurtling bombs to bring all that grey and quiet-seeming front to an instant uproar of smoke and flame, spurting red veins into the sky from the arcs of the answering tracer.

The time was exactly ten minutes past five o'clock.

The leading craft were then less than one thousand yards offshore, and as the aircraft swerved up and away from their brief assault the guns of the destroyers opened fire to set the whole promenade ablaze and fill the sky above the landing craft with the curious quiet shuffle of shells.

For five minutes that harsh and sibilant music filled the ears of two thousand men crouched ready and waiting for the ramps to go down, and for the rasp of stones that would send them rushing over that shingle bank to storm the wall.

The last half mile narrowed swiftly to two hundred yards. Three red Very lights from the leading craft signalled the destroyers, and the barrage switched at once to the flanks, leaving more than a score of tall buildings burning behind the Boulevard de Verdun.

With two hundred yards to go, the support landing craft began to lob their smoke bombs to veil all the fringe of the sea. The dawn was shattered now. The silence was ended. Through the smoke and into the guns the assault craft reached that one thousand seven hundred yard long curving arc of beach, and deployed upon it from end to end, from the wooden breakwater of the West Jetty in the East to the West headland.

Then the enemy guns roared out, suddenly to drench all the

sea approaches and the foreshore with a deluge of fire that tore the water to frayed shreds of wild spray.

Behind them and in front of them as they landed, the wild uproar of the guns enclosed the Canadians in a terrible cage of din and death from which somehow they must break out.

The time was twenty-three minutes past five o'clock. They were three minutes late.

2

A terrific battle raged at once on the sea fringe as the Royal Hamiltons charged out of their landing craft to struggle for a foothold on that bleak desolation of stones fenced with its deep barriers of wire. In those first moments the flak and support landing craft joined with the gun boats, motor launches and destroyers, to pour fire into the enemy positions in an attempt to cover the infantry while the smoke held over the East headland. In that opening outburst of fire the crews of the little ships threw caution to the winds to rise to heights of courage and audacity that they were to sustain throughout the long-drawn-out hours of the morning. They were hopelessly outgunned, sitting ducks in the drifting veils of the smoke-screens from which they emerged like Davids to confront the monstrous Goliath of the defence with their puny weapons. From one point alone near to the Casino four 3.7 cm. and one 4.7 cm. anti-tank gun with a range of 9,000 yards fired point blank over open sights. A 10.5 cm. gun-howitzer added the weight of its fire from the same area, while from the West headland, Hindenburg, and from a hundred unidentifiable points a deluge of heavy, medium and light machine-gun fire weaving in with the light A/A batteries,[1] wrought dreadful havoc and confusion.

The tank landing craft, attempting to close the beaches with their ramps down and their doors open, and meeting the full force of the heavier weapons, were stricken like wounded animals to wallow in the shallow water, their ramp chains cut, their hulls riddled with the penetrating fire of armour-piercing and high-explosive shells. Yet with a terrible persistence they crawled in while men remained alive upon them.

[1] Many light A/A guns had dual-purpose roles.

Worse was yet to come as the smoke cleared, meanwhile the mortars and the machine-guns combined with the brilliant deadly sniping to make a death-trap of the beach as the Royal Hamiltons were caught in the open. Yet in face of that bombardment, spurred on by the courage they knew at their backs, the Royal Hamiltons began to cut and blast their ways through the heavy wire barriers. Many men in that assault were bewildered and confused by the sheer force of the reception, but swiftly those who lived began to fight, to answer with rifles and Brens the deluge that poured upon them.

Within ten minutes of the touchdown the Beach Assault Groups, many of them trying to land from the crippled tank landing craft, died in scores. Of seventy-one men of one group of sappers only nine survived, and of those four were wounded. Out of a total strength of eleven officers and three hundred and fourteen other ranks of the Royal Canadian Engineers, nine officers and one hundred and eighty men were killed or wounded at the moment of landing. Thus at the outset the power of the assault force to demolish their targets was gravely curtailed.

Very few coherent voices speak out of that landing. Private Prince of C Company of the Royal Hamiltons is one of them:

'When we landed we were confused for some time but finally got down and began to return some of the fire. We encountered barbed wire and began cutting it. We found it could be crossed without cutting. I tried to go under the last two strands but got hung up. Corporal J. Hartnett was also hung up and was wounded. I think the German sniper is a real specialist. They are wonderful shots and go for the officers and N.C.O.'s. We found that they are mostly planted on roofs or in very high buildings.

'The Germans seemed to be able to lay down mortar bombs where they damned well pleased. The beach was well covered by L.M.G.'s from the buildings and by Heavy and Medium M.G.'s from our flanks.

'After we got over the wire we got down behind the beach wall and were forced to stay there. Going up that wall four of our N.C.O.'s were put out of action. Our Platoon officer was also wounded then. Major C. G. Pirie crawled up and told us to stay put. He got the Colonel on the "18 set" and gave our position and the Colonel told him to stay there. Colonel Labatt was asking the Air Force to bomb the hotels further on. A tank appeared at this moment and after changing direction finally got on the beach. It got a couple of men who were too slow in moving. The tank was hit at this point three times in the tracks and twice just below the turret by some sort of A/Tk gun. The tank after a few attempts turned round and returned the fire. We stayed in this position until time for withdrawal when we organized parties to help wounded. I would like to mention an act of bravery I saw—the man concerned being Private G. McRichie. He is now missing. McRichie was himself quite safe from fire behind the wall we got to. He looked back and saw Corporal Hartnett who was hung on the wire. George (Private McRichie) got a pair of wire cutters and walked out into that heavy M.G. fire and cut the Corporal loose. He then began to roll him through the remainder of the wire and brought him back into the shelter of the wall.'

Even in the first half hour before the smoke cleared from the formidable bulk of the eastern headland, Bismarck, it was plain that the attempt to seize the beaches in one bold stroke must fail. Without the Sappers the sea wall could not be breached. Without the covering fire of the tanks in close support the infantry were almost as helpless as men with bows and arrows. Yet after the first moments of confusion they rallied to fight back. With Bangalores and wire cutters they breached the wire while many men struggled over and under the barriers, firing into the yawning cavity of Dieppe as they crawled over the stones. There were very few gaps in that carefully laid pattern of direct and enfilade fire, but in the face of it the Royal Hamiltons reached the wall, and behind them came six tanks that had got ashore in the first wave, climbing, skidding and swerving over the steep shingle. Of these six, five clawed their ways over the wall, and the sixth climbed the broad steps of the Casino to reach the esplanade. Flying the yellow pennant of C Squadron three moved off at full speed along the Boulevard Marechal Foch. Two more got into positions on the esplanade east of the Casino, and began at once to shell machine-gun posts and anti-tank guns on the West headland. The sixth tank was caught in a tank trap on the esplanade and its crew died fighting. Seven more tanks were stuck on the edge of the sea, four of them disabled, and three of them with cold engines trying to warm up while fighting their guns with great determination, but unable to withstand the battering that engulfed them.

Nevertheless the partial success of the six tanks in reaching the esplanade had given some cover to the right flank of the Royal Hamiltons, and small groups of determined men were quick to take advantage of the chance to move.

All this time the fighters and fighter-bombers of the R.A.F. dived incessantly upon the enemy. It was in vain. At six o'clock, as the smoke cleared from the East headland the enemy played his trump card. At that same moment the gun boat *Locust* was trying to probe the outer defences of the harbour to lead in the Chasseurs, and the second wave of tank landing craft were struggling to close the beach. These met the full force of the terrific armament hidden in the East headland caves. All available destroyers, and *Locust*, turned their guns upon the headland in an endeavour to quell this new fury. It was hopeless. Guns of heavy calibre, probably 88's and 75's, came forward to fire, and immediately withdrew out of sight, invulnerable to guns or the bombs of the R.A.F.[1]

The official record reads as follows:

'This appalling enfilade fire made the capture of the beach impossible and all the rest of the plan fell to the ground.'

By six o'clock two companies of the R.H.L.I. should have been joining with the South Saskatchewan Regiment in attacks against the light A/A batteries, the Goering battery, and in the assault against Quatre Vents Farm, while a third company should have joined with one company of the Essex Scottish to hold the Dieppe perimeter. But the R.H.L.I. were no longer a battalion measured in companies, platoons and sections. Units were shattered out of recognition, most of the leaders were killed or wounded, cohesion was lost. The battalion had become simply small groups of men ready to take and to accept leadership wherever they could find it. Some of these groups were prepared

[1] Constant air reconnaissance and daring low-level photographic sorties had failed to reveal the secrets of the caves in the East headland. And they had not been imagined.

to do more than sell their lives dearly. A few there were hemmed in under the cover of the wall who could do little, but many more were resolved to harry the enemy wherever they could find him. If the battle could not be won, at least there were many ways in which it might be lost.

The Casino was the first objective. Two groups of men following Capt. Hill and Sergeant Hickson, D.C.M., went in to the attack. Lt. Bell led a third group into the town, while yet a fourth group under an unknown officer attempted to storm the West headland. This officer was seen to fall when half-way up the cliff, and there on the cliff all that group perished.

3

The mile-long beach of Dieppe sweeps away from the East headland and the harbour in a south-westerly direction, broadening like the blade of a scimitar. The Essex Scottish Regiment landed up near the 'hilt' where the beach has a depth of approximately 180 yards at high tide. This did not confer any benefit upon them. Instead they met a weight of fire no whit less than that which greeted the Royal Hamilton Light Infantry on the broad expanse of White Beach, and it was concentrated in a narrower and more devastating field. High velocity artillery fired from concealed positions in the fortified hotels and houses behind the Boulevard de Verdun. Mortars used as howitzers responded instantly to the directions of the Forward Observation Officers using field telephones from their covered positions behind the sea wall. The cross-fire of machine-guns firing from innumerable fortified positions was fully co-ordinated with the mortars, the A/A guns with dual-purpose roles, and the 4.7 cm. anti-tank guns in pill-boxes three to four feet thick, and embedded deeply in the ground.

Yet in the brief interval while the smoke-screen still blinded the gunners in the East headland to their targets the Essex Scottish landed, and supported most bravely from the sea, many reached the wall.

In attempting to give a true picture of this succession of events, I find myself imprisoned by their terrible similarity in a narrow framework of words. Men land from landing craft; the beaches are of stones varying from three to six inches in diameter; sea walls, cliffs and headlands enclose them. And within these confines, almost devoid of cover, men are enfiladed by merciless fire and slaughtered in droves. These things beat upon my mind like the strokes of a hammer, day after day. But there is no way out. I must pursue this repetition, seeking constantly to curb the use of words such as 'heroism', 'courage', 'devastating', 'fury' that spring constantly to the end of my pen. Yet even the official record of these events is at times unable to avoid the purple phrase. These things happened. In their emphasis the tragedy may emerge the more starkly.

When they landed on Red Beach the Essex Scottish rushed the first of the wire barriers, flinging themselves down upon it, making bridges of their bodies that their fellows might cross. In that first deluge of fire men knew instinctively that there was no time for wire cutting, and that only by sheer speed might the battalion hope to reach the wall. There was no shelter, save only the shallow folds of the shingle. While many charged the wire others burrowed in the loose stones and began to return the enemy fire with rifles and Brens, and thus to give some cover to those advancing. In their wake the mortar detachments and some of the machine-gunners of the Toronto Scottish with their guns on A/A mountings, strove to land and set up their weapons. One mortar detachment lived long enough to direct a score or more of bombs against enemy positions before the Forward Observation Officers under their cowlings directed shells upon them. The 'average life' of static elements upon that beach was measured in a handful of seconds.

Meanwhile officers and N.C.O.'s, the individual prey of snipers, led on towards the wall, many of them maintaining their impetus while suffering mortal wounds, ready only to die when the first objective might be gained. Among these Lt. D. Green, with one foot blown off by mortar fire within a few seconds of landing, led his men a further hundred yards hobbling on the bleeding stump until a second mortar bomb killed him.

The courage with which Lt.-Colonel F. K. Jasperson led his men is amply testified, but he could not lead them beyond the wall. The role of his battalion had dwindled to this. And there, under that shallow and dangerous barrier, the Essex Scottish fought like animals snarling in a trap. Some of them did more.

C.S.M. Stapleton with twelve men hurling grenades into the grenade pits of the enemy, crossed the wall, the esplanade and gardens, to gain the houses. These few, moving fast in the rear of the hotels lining the Boulevard de Verdun, entered two houses in the town. Firing from the windows for more than an hour they engaged enemy patrols, killing many, before by a miracle of retreat they rejoined their harassed comrades.

The East headland had long since emerged from the veils of smoke to withstand easily the repeated attacks of cannon Hurricanes and fighters and the bombardment of the destroyers. There was no help and little hope for the Essex Scottish. Under the wall, suffering constant casualties, they settled down to fight to the end.

From first to last a wireless operator of 'C' Company maintained contact with Brigadier Southam, at first on White Beach, and later on in the Casino. The incessant crackle of fire in the headphones told as clearly as words of the conditions under which the Essex Scottish were holding out.

4

It had been planned to land four troops of tanks in the first wave; two troops to assist in subduing the armed trawlers in the harbour; two troops to help clear White Beach and silence light anti-aircraft guns, and then to help in the capture of the Goering battery and Quatre Vents Farm. Three scout cars were to go with Tank Battalion Headquarters, and remain with 6th Infantry Brigade Headquarters. These headquarters with signallers and the beach signalling party were to be established at St. Remy Church in Dieppe and share with the 4th Infantry Brigade landing at Red Beach. With the tank landing craft were also the sappers to demolish the sea wall and let the tanks through.

The first flight of six tank landing craft of Group 8 were less than five minutes behind time when they began to close the beach. The East headland was still masked in smoke, while Dieppe itself was barely visible beyond the swirling chaos of smoke, a cauldron brewing with the appalling din of war, and festooned with the red ribbons of tracer in monstrous profusion.

Two hundred yards out the tank landing craft met the full force of the anti-tank and light anti-aircraft guns sited and ranged especially to meet them as they emerged to close the beach. Even as the infantry on the beaches met the full force of mortars and machine-guns in the first moment of assault, so also these tank landing craft met the full force of the heavier weapons.

In the face of this great weight of fire the lightly armed supporting vessels, disdaining the protection of smoke, closed in to point-blank range in their attempts to cover the tanks. On the tank landing craft the machine-gunners of the Toronto Scottish in exposed positions offered themselves as sacrifices, manning and fighting their guns until they died.

Shuddering to the frightful impact of fire the landing craft crept on over that brief stretch of sea. It seemed that not one of them could hope to reach the shore, still less to loose their burdens upon the enemy. The ramp chains of two were cut, the ramps swinging and folding back under the hulls.

The Tank Landing Craft 145, hit in a dozen places, yet with her ramp intact, touched down successfully and landed three tanks. It was her last desperate effort. Hit again as she tried to draw away she drifted broadside on to the beach and sank fifty yards out.

Next to her the Tank Landing Craft 127 forced her way in with her ramp smashed, and with her engine-room, her ammunition and magazine all on fire, her crew almost all dead or wounded. But a rating still lived at her helm, and two gunners of the Toronto Scottish manned their guns as the tanks crawled out of the burning oven the vessel had become.

The third craft with her ramp chains cut and her doors jammed stuck helpless on the beach. A fourth got in on fire, unloaded her tanks, and sank in shallow water. A fifth landed her tanks and struggled out from the beach for sixty or seventy yards before she lost way, and wallowed helpless and sinking.

At the last came Tank Landing Craft 163 fighting a dogged battle with disaster. Early on she had been hit in the engine-room and had caught fire. A moment afterwards the vessel veered sharply to port as the helmsman collapsed, overcome by fumes. At once a naval rating took the helm, and brought the vessel round head on before a direct hit killed him. A third rating took his place, and the distance narrowed in a kind of slow motion to seventy yards before this helmsman also died. A fourth rating then brought Tank Landing Craft 163 to the beach to land her tanks, and with the same rating at the helm of the burning vessel she pulled away from the beach, making a bold attempt to take the sinking craft in tow. In this she failed, but it seemed that the enemy had done his worst to her, and miraculously Tank Landing Craft 163 made her own way out to sea.

There were seventeen tanks on shore as a result of this brave endeavour, and six of them reached the esplanade. Of these, the three that had gone off at speed in a westerly direction along the Boulevard Marechal Foch flying the yellow pennant of 'C Squadron', little is known. A tank commanded by Lt. W. C. Patterson knocked down a house. Another was seen in the Rue Grande. At least two tanks finally made their way back to the beach with all their ammunition gone. No man lived to tell of their exploits.

There were many unlooked-for tank obstacles, especially on the Boulevard de Verdun, that had not been revealed by air photography. By day the enemy had removed all trace, and had hidden his anti-tank guns. These reappeared each night at dusk, and were removed at dawn. Road blocks protected all the entrances to the town and promenade. These were eight feet high and four feet thick, with sloping backs on which fire-steps had been built.

Of the tanks on the beach two lost their tracks, one lost its turret, and a fourth had the turret badly damaged. An officer climbed out of this tank with one of his eyes shot out, and ran at once to a second tank following up behind. He climbed in, and a moment later this tank knocked out the gun that had wounded him.

But none of these, lurching and floundering, burrowing grooves in the loose shingle, and in the face of deadly fire, reached the wall. Nevertheless they fought to the last, and gave some cover to the Royal Hamiltons in their fight for the Casino.

Meanwhile throughout the landing the large flak landing craft, commanded by Lt. E. L. Graham, R.N.V.R., was conspicuous, closing the beach to attack the enemy at point-blank range. One by one the guns were fought until they were put out of action and the gunners killed. When the Captain was killed, Surgeon-Lt. M. P. Martin, M.R.C.S., the only surviving officer, took command and fought the ship until she sank under him. By so doing he afforded some protection to the four tank landing craft of the second flight.

This medical officer was finally rescued, wounded, from the sea and put aboard *Calpe*. There, throughout the day, despite his own condition, he tended the wounded.

5

The smoke had cleared from the East headland as the four tank landing craft of the second flight came in exactly on time at five minutes past six o'clock. They carried with them not only tanks, but also Brigadier Lett and Staff Officers of the 4th Infantry Brigade, together with Lt.-Colonel Parks-Smith, R.M., of Combined Operations Headquarters, in command of the Beach Provost Party, and Lt.-Colonel J. G. Andrews, commanding the 14th Canadian Army Tank Battalion of the Calgary Highlanders.

These officers were on board Tank Landing Craft 125, to which Lt.-Colonel Andrews had transferred offshore, coming in slightly astern and to starboard of Tank Landing Craft 214. These two craft met the full weight of the barrage unleashed at that moment out of the caves of the East headland. Nevertheless, No. 214, brought almost to a standstill by direct hits, closed the beach in a sinking condition to land her tanks under a tremendous concentration of fire.

This was the target the enemy had longed for and waited for, and a great number of guns were designed and ranged for this purpose. As soon as her cargo was landed No. 214 crawled away almost along the sea bed, holed like a sieve, and to sink as soon as she was out of her depth.

The Tank Landing Craft 125 with her cargo of commanders and tanks had gained some slight cover in the lee of the stricken vessel. She managed to close the beach and get one tank away before she met the full force of the enemy fire, and then in one burst with her crew killed or wounded it seemed that she must be overwhelmed. The vessel was no longer head on to the beach, and those among the wounded who could still move got some way on her astern, trying then to square her up for a second attempt.

The stricken craft had become a vortex of fire, her crew out of action as she drifted again towards the beach. Brigadier Lett had suffered severe wounds, and Lt.-Colonel Parks-Smith lay mortally wounded and dying by his side. At this stage, Lt.-Colonel

Andrews, seeing his hopes of getting ashore to take command of the tanks rapidly fading, decided to get away. The vessel was only a few yards offshore, her ramp down and damaged by shell fire that threatened to cut it loose at any moment. It must have seemed to Andrews that he was unlikely to gain another yard. His tank was already out on the damaged ramp, and with a sudden lurch it left the ship and was drowned in eight feet of water. The tanks had been water-proofed to a depth of six feet.

Like men escaping from the hatch of a submarine just above water, the crew climbed out and swam for the beach. At the last Lt.-Colonel Andrews climbed from the hatch, paused for a moment to look round, and was heard to shout: "I'm baling out," before jumping into the sea.

A motor launch, swooping in with her guns blazing in an attempt to cover and rescue the survivors, picked up the Colonel and was immediately engulfed in flames from a seeming deluge of direct hits. It is probable that all on board were killed in that instant before the motor launch sank in the shallows.

Meanwhile Tank Landing Craft 125 was still afloat, and those alive on board were fighting to save her and the wounded. A Sergeant of Royal Marines had at once cut the ramp cables after the loss of the second tank and the last of the crew. The Sergeant then took the helm. In the engine-room Major M. E. P. Garneaux, a Staff Officer of 4th Infantry Brigade, had reversed the engines, and immediately afterwards manned a pompom.

Slowly, crawling astern, the Royal Marine Sergeant at the helm spotted the engineer struggling to regain the vessel from the water. He had been blown overboard by blast, but was unhurt. Major Garneaux got him back on board, and he at once took charge of the engines. In such fashion the vessel gained the cover of the outer smoke-screens protecting the heart of the convoy, and was taken in tow by a motor launch to safety.

The remaining two landing craft had fought their way in to land their tanks, but with little success. The third vessel, covered to some extent from the full weight of fire from the East headland by the two vessels almost abeam on her port side, landed her tanks without a hitch. Within two minutes all three gained the wall, only to founder there, unable to grip the shingle and to climb to the esplanade.

On that desolation of shifting stones, swept by a fiendish

pattern of gunfire no armoured vehicle could withstand, the tanks had the aspect of unwieldy wounded beasts, seeming to flounder almost blindly as they strove to bring their guns to bear upon the targets on the headlands.

Tank Landing Craft 165, the fourth in line, also reached the beach, but the fortune of her tanks was worse. The first tank stalled on the beach, and was an easy prey for enemy guns. The second tank fouled an airduct, and caught fire from a direct hit within a minute of landing. The third tank fouled the port side of the door, and was hit while still on the ramp.

This was a position of the utmost danger for the tank and the vessel, and then with a roar the engine started, and the tank lurched off violently into the sea, pushing the landing craft astern and dragging a scout car after her through four feet of water. The driver of the scout car hung on, swaying wildly in his small vehicle in the wake of the tank as it roared over the shingle, and on up over the sea wall to the esplanade in one great bound. There the scout car got free and moved off at full speed along the Boulevard Marechal Foch, while the tank fought like a beast at bay, pouring fire into the hotels and boarding houses that were now wreathed in smoke and flames.

This was the last tank to cross the wall. Of the twenty-four tank landing craft which had sailed, ten landed a total of twenty-eight tanks. Seven of these crossed the wall. One was drowned. Twenty were swiftly casualties. All were lost.

The remaining fourteen tank landing craft of the third and fourth waves, due to go in to land at intervals up to a final landing at ten o'clock, awaited offshore the order to land. It was never given.

All these craft were equipped with barrage balloons to defend them from air attack. In the event no balloons were flown. The R.A.F. controlled the air above all that battleground on land and sea, as yet unchallenged by enemy bombers. Had it been otherwise the shambles of the beaches might well have been matched by the shambles of the sea.

Through all that day the pennant of Lt.-Colonel Andrews flew from the turret of his drowned tank, a forlorn symbol in an aching void of desolation as the tide receded to leave the tank high and dry on the smooth sands beyond the stones.

CHAPTER TWELVE

THE FLOATING RESERVE

I

THE landing of the Fusiliers Mont-Royal, the Floating Reserve, commanded by Lt.-Colonel D. Ménard, took place at four minutes past seven o'clock at points one thousand yards and more westward of Red Beach. It was a disaster.

Emerging from smoke-screens laid by destroyers, the landing craft found themselves one hundred yards offshore confronting the western end of White Beach, and half of them under the unscalable cliffs of the West headland. At once the sea erupted like a boiling cauldron, gushing great spouts of water, whipped by a hurricane of shot and shell. It was too late to turn back. They went in to land: there was no choice.

Three hundred officers and men got in on a narrow beach under the bulk of the West headland to find themselves marooned. They were wedged into a narrow no-man's-land from which there was no escape. The remainder of the battalion landed strung out over the desolate wilderness of tangled wire, smoking and derelict tanks, and broken stones that White Beach had become, and swept by pitiless enemy fire constantly thickened up by the arrival of new mortars firing like howitzers.

Reduced almost at once to no more than a shattered rump of a battalion the survivors took what cover they could find in the folds of the shingle, threw up stone barriers round themselves, sought cover behind the few tanks spaced out over that awful shambles of foreshore, forsaken by all save themselves and the battered dead.

Overhead the sky had clouded, adding to the greyness of this grim prospect. Broken strands of wire curled into the air in grotesque shapes festooned with the limp bodies of men like puppets flung carelessly aside. And all round, laced with the tracer of the machine-guns, smoke rose incessantly as from a burned-out patch. There the remnants of the Fusiliers Mont-Royal lay down to fight until they died.

Soon after six o'clock the Military Force Commander had decided to commit his Floating Reserve to the support of Red Beach. The messages received at that hour from Brigadier Lett and Lt.-Colonel Andrews, stating that they were about to land, had seemed reassuring. The Military Force Commander could not know that these messages had preceded by a few minutes the severe wounds of Brigadier Lett and the death of Lt.-Colonel Andrews.

As we have already noted, information was sketchy in the extreme, much of it of doubtful source, or non-existent. Blue Beach was a blank, a vacuum that might yet be filled with victory or disaster, yet somehow without promise. It seemed that the one outstanding need above all others was that the East headland, Bismarck, must be secured at all costs. Without that the raid must fail in its main material purposes.

Accordingly the Fusiliers Mont-Royal, embarked in twenty-six large personnel landing craft, led by Lt.-Commander J. H. Dathan, R.N., set course for Red Beach under cover of smoke. Two of the landing craft were lost by gunfire on the way in, but the smoke-screens in the main masked the approach effectively up to the last moments. Unfortunately they had also inevitably masked Dieppe itself from view.

At any time up to six o'clock that would not have mattered, but meanwhile the tide had taken a strong westerly set, and this was an unexpected and unobserved factor unknown to Lt.-Commander Dathan at the head of the column. Forced to navigate blind through the smoke, and without a chance of a landfall until it was too late, the landing craft missed Red Beach by more than one thousand yards with the left flank, and was off the beach entirely on the extreme right.

Lt.-Colonel Ménard, landing with the main body in the centre, was at once severely wounded. Gaining the shelter of a tank he strove to direct and inspire his men. Officers and N.C.O.'s struggled bravely to lead on, but most were forced to the shingle. They had suffered gravely at the moment of landing. A battalion had become little more than a scattered company, lacking aims other than to hit back as best they could at an enemy hidden behind powerful defences.

Ahead of them they could see small groups of men of the Royal Hamilton Light Infantry engaging the gunners of the Casino with their rifles and Brens, and working in towards the flanks of the building. Others were firing steadily from positions against the sea wall. Two tanks were still in action on the esplanade, and in these things the Mont-Royal found some hope.

Lt. P. P. Loranger, severely wounded at the touchdown, strove to lead the remnant of his platoon onward to the wall. Forced to the meagre shelter of the stones he held his men together, denying a passive role, and covering with controlled and effective fire the fierce assaults of three small bands of men going in to the attack.

Out of the chaos and confusion of the landing three men had towered above their fellows, and had rallied many to follow them. These three men were Capt. Vandeloe, Sergeant-Major Dumais and Sergeant Dubuc. They were men of rare quality, seeming larger than life even in the bald official record of their deeds. There were no orders now. No battalion. These three, assuming leadership of all who would follow, went in to fight in their various ways, determined to come to grips with the enemy, and to tear him out from behind his guns.

Capt. Vandeloe leading a score of men, and covered by Lt. Loranger's party from the folds of the shingle, stormed up and over the sea wall. Some little way to his right Sergeant-Major Dumais led a smaller group into the attack against the Casino to join with the Royal Hamiltons and Sappers resolved on the same purpose.

Meanwhile Sergeant Dubuc had landed with his men at a point opposite the western end of the Casino. He had taken in something of the plight of half the battalion under the West headland, yet with no means of knowing that they were trapped. Dubuc's first aim was to liquidate as many enemy guns as possible covering what might be the exit from under the headland. It was the kind of situation for which such men seem to have been born, and which others recognize instinctively in a crisis. With an utter disregard of danger, careless even of whether or not others were with him, Dubuc rushed upon two pill-boxes threatening his immediate front, and overwhelmed them almost, it seemed, with his bare hands.

The diversion of the landing, coupled with the sudden bold attacks of these small parties of the Mont-Royals, had aided the Royal Hamiltons under Capt. A. C. Hill and C.S.M. J. Stewart, to press home simultaneous flanking attacks against the Casino. While riflemen engaged a heavy machine-gun firing from a top north-east window, Sappers captured and destroyed two concrete pill-boxes with Bangalore torpedoes and killed the garrisons. These pill-boxes had blocked the approach to the courtyard, and at once Hill and Stewart led charges under the light machine-guns and took the Casino by assault.

At the same time Sergeant G. E. Hickson broke in with a party of Sappers from the rear, and exploded a three pound plastic charge to bring twenty-three Germans out of hiding to surrender. The Sappers then blew up the guns.

It was twelve minutes past seven o'clock when this success rewarded two hours of relentless fighting, and opened up a way into the town.

All this time a small nucleus of Brigade Headquarters staff with Major H. F. Lazier and Capt. J. M. Currie had organized the kernel of a Headquarters round Brigadier Southam, commanding the 6th Canadian Infantry Brigade from a precarious position under the wall. Throughout the morning Brigadier Southam had held a tenuous thread of communication rather than command over the whole front, the sole focal point of contact with the Headquarters ship H.M.S. *Calpe*.

As soon as the Casino fell, the Brigadier made a dash for the building with his signallers, while Major Lazier and Capt. Currie began to organize all-round defence, using the slit trenches on the south, abandoned by the enemy.

Sergeant-Major Dumais, fighting his way through with his small party, manned the defensive posts on the second floor, and at once Brigadier Southam signalled his news that the Casino had fallen.

Meanwhile Capt. Hill and C.S.M. Stewart had pressed on to cross the Boulevard Marechal Foch and the gardens. They had no very clear plan in mind save only to come to grips with the enemy on equal terms behind his guns, and to destroy whatever installations they could lay their hands on. Fighting their way round a well-sited road block at the western end of the Boulevard de Verdun both parties reached a cinema, pausing there to assess their situation, and decide on courses open to them.

Sergeant Hickson had also led his party of Sappers into the town, attacking houses, tearing out electrical installations and telegraph wires, and firing warehouses. In the course of these operations civilians wearing white arm-bands fired upon them, and warned enemy patrols, but Hickson and his men more than held their own against all whom they met.

The French by that time had been warned, by broadcasts and pamphlets distributed from the air, that this was a raid and not an invasion, and to remain indoors. Doubtless all but the boldest would have remained indoors anyway.

It had been forecast by Military Intelligence that 1,700 enemy troops might be expected to hold Dieppe up to three hours after the landing, together with ancillary troops manning the defences. In the matter of numbers they were correct, and the enemy were of poor quality, provided by 571 Infantry Regiment of 302 Division, and not by 110 Division as had been forecast. It was of no great importance.

At that time Lt. L. C. Bell of the Royal Hamiltons, one of the first to get off the beach, had been marauding to some purpose in the town with a handful of men for a full hour, attacking patrols and inflicting numerous casualties on the enemy at various points. He had reached St. Remy Church, hoping to find Brigade Headquarters established and link up with an effective force, but finding the church deserted he returned to the Casino to make contact with the Command soon after the other parties had gone off into the town.

Lt. Bell was welcomed, and his men at once manned the slit trenches facing the town and guarding the rear of the Casino building.

At about that time the guns of *Albrighton*, well directed by a Forward Observation officer who had somehow got in behind Red Beach, repeatedly hit the tobacco factory and fired it, while an unknown party of Sappers succeeded in destroying the Gas Works. There was not then, and there is not now, any means of knowing just how many small parties of men succeeded in penetrating into Dieppe to take some toll of the enemy before they died.

Meanwhile, Sergeant Dubuc had looked for new fields to conquer immediately after destroying the pill-boxes. He appreciated at once that the guns of the West headland, scarcely less formidable, though more vulnerable, than those hidden in the East headland, were a constant threat to the Royal Hamiltons and to the remnants of his own battalion with his wounded Colonel. At that moment the pennant of Lt.-Colonel Andrews, flying from the drowned tank, caught his attention.

The tank had been left high and dry on the sand by the fast ebbing tide, and Dubuc realized from its position that it must have fallen off the ramp of its landing craft, and that its guns and ammunition might be intact. Without hesitation, beckoning one man to his side, Dubuc bounded off over the stones and the widening fringe of hard sand beyond, running like a stag with his mate at his heels. Together they gained the tank, and from that small isolated fortress on the edge of the sea Dubuc turned his guns upon the West headland, fighting under the pennant of the Calgary Highlanders until his ammunition was exhausted, and at least six machine-gun posts and anti-tank guns had ceased to fire.

Throughout this almost private battle with the guns of the West headland, Dubuc had tried to observe the condition of the three hundred lost officers and men of the Mont-Royals. It was clear now that their position was hopeless. They were without orders. Their wireless sets were all out of order. One hundred of their number had suffered wounds coming in to land, many of them grave. Faced by unscalable cliffs, they had at last tried to work round the flank of the headland westward, hoping to reach Green Beach and join up with the South Saskatchewan Regiment and the Queen's Own Cameron Highlanders. But they found the way blocked and impassable. There was no better prospect to the east; no outlet to White Beach without swimming, impossible except perhaps for a few fortunate individuals. There was no room to manœuvre; no room even to fight. Their only hope was that in the hour of withdrawal their plight might be realized.

When Dubuc had reached the stranded tank and opened up against the headland there were still two tanks in action on the esplanade; one of these had covered the sortie of Sergeant Hickson, and was trying to save ammunition in the hope of performing similar services to others. There were tanks also in the town doing whatever damage presented possibilities to their guns.

Just after half past seven o'clock a party of Sappers with the Royal Hamiltons had succeeded in breaching the sea wall near the Casino. The breach was too late, for there were no tanks on the beach capable of movement or even of firing a shot.

A message received on board *Calpe*, and purporting to come

from Brigadier Southam, gave the news of the breach in the wall and stated that the tanks had been ordered through. This message was misleading, and in conjunction with other fragmentary messages constantly coming in, almost certainly from enemy sources, the Military Force Commander was getting a picture of White Beach a great deal better than the facts.

One message at this time asked for bombing on a part of the West headland, but the operator when challenged could not give the code word previously arranged, and the message was discounted.

Nevertheless it would have been difficult to avoid a growing impression that progress was being made, and the deteriorating weather and very poor visibility made it impossible for the Force Commanders at sea to get any kind of direct view.

But it was certain that the South Saskatchewan Regiment were fighting strongly in Pourville on the West flank of the West headland, Hindenburg, and it seemed that swift and strong support at this critical time might enable infantry to win the West headland, and the Sappers to accomplish many demolitions.

From the messages it appeared that the Royal Hamiltons had, in fact, captured part of the headland.

A further factor involved the difficult problems of withdrawal that must soon be faced. Under the appalling enfilade fire from the two headlands withdrawal might well be a disaster even worse than the landings. Success against the West headland might therefore save hundreds of lives, and snatch some success to lighten the darkening shadow of defeat.

Soon after seven o'clock the Military Force Commander reached a decision to reinforce White Beach with his one remaining reserve force, the Royal Marines. All subsequent messages served to confirm the wisdom of this decision. At seventeen minutes past eight o'clock a message was received stating that White Beach was under control and the tanks were making progress. The Royal Marines were going in to land. It looked well.

CHAPTER THIRTEEN

THE ROYAL MARINE COMMANDO

THE decision to reinforce White Beach with the Royal Marine Commando had been reached by the Military Force Commander, Major-General H. F. Roberts, in conference with the Naval Force Commander, Capt. J. Hughes-Hallett, R.N., and Commander J. E. D. Ryder, V.C., R.N. Commander Ryder had been in charge of the cutting-out party on board H.M.S. *Locust*, and soon after seven o'clock, having reported the impossibility of that enterprise, he was ordered to collect as many landing craft as possible, and then to tranship the Royal Marines into them from their Chasseurs. This in itself was an operation demanding considerable skill and resource.

The scene at sea off Dieppe had become one of seething activity, with a great bustle of small ships hurrying in and out of the smoke-screens like shadows, to the incessant accompaniment of gunfire and the roar of the fighter aircraft overhead.

A Boat Pool had been formed under cover of smoke laid by support craft, and into this the landing craft of all sizes continuously assembled and set forth as they came and went upon their dangerous missions.

From five o'clock in the morning small craft had been bringing back their wounded, and those few they had been able to save from time to time from the beaches. The naval crews had suffered very heavily at the landings, many men remaining at their posts with first-aid dressings on their wounds.

By eight o'clock there were already more than two hundred and fifty casualties being cared for on board *Calpe*, in addition to at least one quarter of her own crew. *Fernie* and others of the destroyers also had their wardrooms full of wounded.

Throughout this whole period *Calpe* and *Fernie*, manœuvring of necessity in narrow orbits in view of their commanding roles, ceaselessly bombarded the enemy positions in support of the main beaches. Destroyers, steam and motor gun boats, motor launches and support vessels of all kinds were continuously engaged in smoke-laying tasks, and in works of rescue, while giving all possible fire support to the men on the beaches, and screening the flanks of the whole expedition from enemy naval interference. Offshore the fourteen tank landing craft of the third and fourth waves awaited with their escorts the orders to land. And now, too, the Air-Sea Rescue launches plied at speed within a three-mile limit rescuing pilots from the sea.

In the midst of all this movement of many ships in the drifting veils of smoke, and under sustained fire from enemy Coastal batteries, Commander Ryder collected and manœuvred his assault landing craft and the Chasseurs, and carried out the transhipment of the Royal Marine Commando with the utmost smoothness. At half past eight o'clock the Commander reported his ships ready to go in to land.

The order was given at once, and then through a series of smoke-screens laid by the destroyers, and covered by the guns of H.M.S. *Locust*, two flak landing craft and the Chasseurs, all in close support, the slender line of assault craft moved in steadily towards the beach. They knew well the high hopes they carried. They knew, too, something of the desperate nature of their venture, and were glad of it, for otherwise they felt that they would have sailed in vain.

Through the smoke, and like a drum-beat undertone to the thunder of the guns, they heard the harsh monotone of the machine-guns and the crump of mortars. But this menacing music bore no more resemblance to the ultimate reality than the plucking of strings bears to the full volume of a symphony orchestra.

Emerging from the smoke the leading craft came at once into full view of the beach and of the enemy. They met the most murderous concentration of fire that had burst upon that fateful morning.

For more than an hour the enemy had been bringing up Field artillery and horse-drawn heavy mortars to support the light anti-aircraft and anti-tank guns, and the great weight of fire from the headlands. In growing alarm, unable to gauge the size of the naval force at sea, the enemy was massing to repel the invasion of which he imagined he had so far seen the spearhead.

In the face of this deluge of high explosive, seamed with the whine of machine-gun and rifle bullets, the assault craft held on, resolved to close the beach. Men stood devoid of cover answering as best they could with rifles and ·Brens as the assault craft were buffeted like fragile corks in the vortex of some fiendish storm.

The official document recording this landing reads simply:

'With a courage terrible to see the Marines went in to land, determined, if fortune so willed, to repeat at Dieppe what their fathers had accomplished at Zeebrugge.'

In the last moments, as the first landing craft touched down on the belt of sand left by the ebbing tide below the stones, Marines Breen and Bradshaw distinguished themselves among the bravest of the brave. Few who reached the shore survived, and of those few were Lt. W. R. Smale and the remains of his platoon. Finding some cover behind a stranded tank landing craft, Lt. Smale was last seen with two N.C.O.'s, all three engaging the enemy machine-guns steadfastly with their Brens.

Meanwhile in the shallows a tragedy was played out to avert a tragedy. In that dreadful moment of revelation as the assault craft came out of the cover of smoke it had been as if a curtain had lifted suddenly upon inferno. Upon the instant Lt.-Colonel J. P. Phillipps, the Commanding Officer, recognized the utter hopelessness of the situation. For himself, and all those with him in the first few vessels, there could be but the merest chance of survival. But for those behind there might be hope. Without a moment's hesitation, and before any man realized his purpose, the Colonel pulled on his white gloves and leapt to the small forward deck to stand upright in face of the enemy. Easily recognizable by his white gloves he was too prominent to be missed either by the enemy or by his men. He had resolved to halt the landing, if it were possible, and save all those who followed. He had but a few seconds to live, and in those seconds with his white-gloved hands above his head, a proud and most noble figure, he signalled, and clearly made his purpose known, to the landing craft to put about and head back into the shelter of the smoke.

For perhaps ten seconds his body remained upright, before he fell mortally wounded to the deck, yet knowing with his last breath, as his men lifted his body, that he had probably saved two hundred men from the murderous fire that must have added their numbers to the final count.

Six landing craft managed at once to turn about on the fringe of the smoke at the Colonel's signal, but the seventh, under Capt. R. R. Devereaux, R.M., remained behind in an attempt to save a few who still lived from one of the sinking vessels. Only then did he turn about to gain the smoke cover with his own assault craft in a sinking condition. The effort would have been in vain had not the Chasseur 43, standing by in close support, gone at once to the rescue to take all on board.

The task of rescue was indeed all that now remained to be done. On the Red and White Beaches, in Dieppe itself, in Pourville, and in the woods behind Green Beach, perhaps three thousand men still lived and fought. Even behind Blue Beach some might still survive.

Everywhere the enemy reinforcements were closing in, and large forces were on the move. The battle could not be won, but all was not yet lost. In the air the R.A.F. remained supreme, still challenging the enemy to fight, and the Navy still ruled the narrow sea.

It was nine o'clock; six hours since the infantry landing ships had put the assault craft into the water.

PART TWO

VANQUISH

CHAPTER FOURTEEN

NINE O'CLOCK

I

THE situation as appreciated by the Naval and Military Force Commanders on board the Headquarters ship H.M.S. *Calpe* at nine o'clock was as follows:

(i) Twenty officers and O.R.'s of No. 3 Commando had withdrawn from Yellow Beach Two at Berneval, and were on their way homeward.

(ii) At Blue Beach, Puits, there were only dead and wounded of the Royal Regiment of Canada.

(iii) On the water front of Dieppe itself, Red and White Beaches, the Essex Scottish Regiment and the Royal Hamilton Light Infantry, were fighting desperately to maintain themselves under a steadily increasing fire. Elements of Royal Hamilton Light Infantry had penetrated into the town a short distance, and Royal Canadian Engineers had set fire to warehouses near the tobacco factory.

The reinforcements of the Fusiliers Mont-Royal and the Royal Marine Commando had suffered too heavily to affect the situation.

Several tanks were still in action, but all mortar detachments had been wiped out.

(iv) The South Saskatchewan Regiment were heavily engaged behind Pourville, Green Beach, trying to take Quatre Vents Farm.

The Queen's Own Cameron Highlanders of Canada were about $2\frac{1}{4}$ miles inland striving to reach the St. Aubin aerodrome.

(v) No. 4 Commando at Vasterival and Varengeville, the Orange Beaches, had successfully completed their tasks, and were on their way back to England.

It was also clear that the situation was deteriorating rapidly, and it was becoming increasingly difficult to close the beaches. At sea the destroyer *Garth* was running out of ammunition, and *Alresford* was towing a damaged tank landing craft away from White Beach. The destroyers *Slazak*, *Brocklesby* and *Bleasdale* had sailed to the North-East to investigate a report that German E-boats were approaching from Boulogne. Of the destroyers only *Albrighton* and *Garth* had made contact with their Forward Observation Officers ashore. The *Albrighton* had fired with great effect, particularly in silencing a light A.A. battery East of the Radar Station at Pourville, and in firing the tobacco factory. All the destroyers, including *Calpe*, had joined in the direct bombardment while their A/A gunners ceaselessly engaged the growing enemy fighter force overhead.

At no time had the fire-power of the destroyers been equal to the task of giving adequate support to the beaches, but now the guns were too light even to challenge the heavy artillery the enemy was bringing steadily forward, and the targets were too well concealed and too well protected.

In the face of this situation the idea that the remaining tanks might be put ashore was finally abandoned, and *Garth*, already with barely a shot in her locker, together with *Alresford*, were ordered to escort the fourteen tank landing craft forming groups 10 and 11 back to England.

All landing craft had by now returned to the Boat Pool, protected by an almost continuous smoke-screen laid by destroyers and support craft.

Soon after nine o'clock, therefore, the Naval Force Commander advised that the withdrawal should take place as soon as possible, and that all material ashore must be abandoned. The Military Force Commander agreed. Capt. Hughes-Hallett had already appreciated that the evacuation of the Red and White Beaches might be impossible, and had sent Commander H. V. P. McClintock, R.N., urgently to Pourville to inform the Beachmaster that Green Beach should not be evacuated and must be held.

The times of withdrawal from the flanking beaches had been previously fixed, and Major-General Roberts now thought that it might be necessary to hold Green Beach open in an attempt to take off the whole force from there.

But in the face of heavy fire, Commander McClintock was unable to close Green Beach, or to reach the Beachmaster with a message. This experience was ominous. The orders could not be given.

It was clear beyond a shadow of doubt on board *Calpe* that withdrawal in the face of these conditions would be an operation of the utmost danger, and that every hour—or even minute—of delay must add to the difficulties and the danger. All the while enemy pressure was increasing, pressing the men in closer upon the narrow beaches to drive them at last out into the open to slaughter under the devastating fire-power massed against them, and upon the way they must go.

Nevertheless, the withdrawal could not be hurried beyond a certain point, for the Royal Air Force, without whose close aid the whole attempt would surely end in disaster, must have time to adjust their complex time-table and to undertake to lay smoke-screens. This could not be before eleven o'clock.

The orders were issued soon after nine o'clock.

Commander McClintock would send all assault landing craft and motor landing craft to the beaches, and these would ferry troops out to tank landing craft standing one mile offshore.

All available destroyers and flak landing craft would give fire support and lay smoke, while the R.A.F. carried out a series of bombing attacks against the East and West headlands, and laid curtains of smoke over the Red and White Beaches.

At twenty-two minutes past ten o'clock the destroyers would form a line 070 degrees to 250 degrees to follow the landing craft in. The wind was already beginning to blow on-shore from the West. It would help.

When these orders had been given those on the beaches and behind the beaches faced the task of fighting for a further two or three hours, culminating in a desperate attempt to regain the landing craft from which they had disembarked in the dawn twilight. The tide by then would have ebbed to the full to widen the gauntlet that must be run. The situation in reverse might prove more devastating than the ordeal of landing, and no man on land or sea had a doubt of it.

2

The original operation of the withdrawal had been planned in detail. It had been hoped to take off 4,250 men, 58 tanks, and other material, from the main beaches over a period of three and one half hours. That operation and the expectation had to be greatly modified. From the minute of zero every succeeding minute would be precious. It might be beyond human power to remain for an hour off the beaches, or even for landing craft to approach. It might be beyond human power to snatch even one thousand men from death. And in that effort many must surely die.

The zero hour was eleven o'clock. The code word, Vanquish.

CHAPTER FIFTEEN

THE WAY BACK

FROM a very early hour the first of the little ships had set off on the journey homeward, feeling their ways through the mine-swept channels soon after dawn. By nine o'clock a score or more were strung out across the sea. It was a journey not without hazard.

Following the unfortunate—and fortuitous—naval clash of the Steam Gun Boat 5 with the German armed trawlers off Berneval, many of the landing craft, finding themselves alone in the total darkness, and unable to make contact, had finally turned back. They carried with them the main body of No. 3 Commando.

Five of the landing craft had failed with engine trouble before reaching the scene of the sea battle. By the time they had got going again it was too late to make an attempt to find the main body. Four others were badly damaged in the landing on Yellow Beach One, and some of those at sea had lost members of their crews, killed and wounded, in that first furious burst of fire from the enemy trawlers. But all save those lost in the brave effort against Yellow Beach One at Berneval were limping homeward across the Channel. Behind them sailed the landing craft commanded by Lt. Buckee with Major Young's gallant party from Yellow Beach Two at Belleville. In that always vulnerable position Buckee's landing craft survived the repeated attempts of a JU. 88 to sink her in mid Channel. The vessel reached port safely.

Of the others, a few were in unaccustomed hands. The crew of the large Personnel Landing Craft 87 had all been killed or severely wounded at a single blow in the first blast of fire from the enemy trawlers, and at once a sergeant of No. 3 Commando had taken the wheel. This man, Sergeant C. E. A. Collins of the Hampshire Regiment, had little navigational knowledge, but he was a man of resource. Alone, as it seemed, on that unwelcoming sea, he took command. For a time he had hoped to fall in with other vessels of the convoy, but at last, steering by his Army prismatic compass, he set a course for England. Half-way across the Channel an Air-Sea Rescue launch gave him a bearing, and he brought the landing craft with its full complement of troops safely into Newhaven.

Meanwhile the victorious No. 4 Commando, returning from the Orange Beaches of Vasterival and Varengeville, having achieved the complete destruction of the Hess battery, approached the main anchorage off Dieppe at the fateful hour of nine o'clock. To the last their operation had gone smoothly. Harassed in the final stages by growing enemy fire the men had regained the landing craft in good order, and as each craft was filled it joined the escorting motor gun boat two miles offshore.

At the time of their arrival at the main anchorage from six to ten landing craft of all kinds bustled round *Calpe* and *Fernie*, and led by the gun boat the landing craft of No. 4 Commando joined the queue for *Fernie* to tranship their wounded. It looked to them, they have recorded, 'like Regatta day at Cowes', which seems a curious description, recalling the calm waters of the Solent gay with bunting under a Summer sun, rather than the smoke and fog, the flash and thunder of gunfire. Perhaps it is a better description of the minds of those men in those hours following their great adventure.

Soon after nine o'clock, No. 4 Commando steered for England at 7 knots. Their good work for the day was not quite done, for they rescued one R.A.F. pilot from the sea, and took two others on board from a motor launch on duty in the minefield.

Behind No. 4 Commando came the tank landing craft of 10 and 11 Groups escorted by *Garth* and *Alresford*, and making a concourse of some fifty little ships all told already under way, while the remainder prepared to meet the final massive challenge of the morning. One tank landing craft was sunk by enemy bombing. All the rest reached home safely.

Long before the processes for the main withdrawal had been set in motion Lt.-Commander Goulding, who had been responsible for the landing of the Royal Regiment of Canada at Puits, had boarded a motor launch, and with Lt.-Commander Mullen in a second launch, had returned to that dreadful scene with grave forebodings. Between them they managed to round up a few landing craft with which to attempt the work of rescue. The visibility meanwhile had become very poor, and the landing craft, led by Goulding with Mullen in support, overshot the narrow bay of Puits. Putting about, the Commander moved slowly Westward and at last picked up the faint silhouette of the valley shrouded in fog and the smoke of gunfire.

Again and again the motor launches and the landing craft strove to run the gauntlet of the enemy guns through that rocky passage to the beach, but they were beaten back by a weight of gunfire that would most certainly have added the crews to the tally of the dead, and destroyed their precious craft. Without adequate fire support the task was hopeless, and the knowledge that it was unlikely that any man remained alive on that beach of Puits did little to lessen the agony of failure. Some hours later a single survivor was picked up at sea.

These brave endeavours had been observed by anxious eyes from above the cliffs where Lt.-Colonel Catto and his small party had contrived to remain hidden. In their dash to evade the German patrol at the time when they had been cut off on the East headland, they had gained the cover of a low wall, and moving at the double through a strip of woodland they had come out on to a road leading to Puits and the church of Notre Dame de Bon Secours. Their position was precarious in the extreme as the whole area was covered by enemy patrols. A scout attempting a reconnaissance in an attempt to find a way through to the beach was killed almost before their eyes. Only then they found that they were within one hundred yards of the gun sites and the battery position that was among the most important objectives of the regiment. They could do nothing.

Twice the small party tried to reach the beach, but they found themselves hemmed in, unable to elude the patrols. It was on these sorties that they saw the landing craft attempting to close the beach, and knew that it was hopeless. It was then after ten o'clock.

Hour after hour they lay hidden while bombers and fighters of the R.A.F. bombed and machine-gunned the gun sites and battery in low-level attacks. But the guns were not silenced. They watched and lay still as a handful of survivors of their regiment were marched along the road from Puits under guard to pass within a few feet of them.

Towards noon the crash and thunder of gunfire rose to its crescendo, filling them with hopes and fears. Then the thunder of the guns died away, fitfully, and at last to silence. For a time the air battle still raged overhead, but it brought little hope. At twenty minutes past four o'clock that afternoon, unable to harry the enemy in any way, the last of their ammunition gone, these few with Lt.-Colonel Catto surrendered.

CHAPTER SIXTEEN

THE FIGHT FOR POURVILLE

I

IT HAD been imperative for the safety and success of the with-drawal from Green Beach that the South Saskatchewan Regiment should hold Pourville village, capture the heights to East and West from which the beach could be dominated, and take Quatre Vents Farm. Without the promised aid of the Royal Hamilton Light Infantry and the tanks, without adequate fire support on land or from the sea, the accomplishment of all these tasks had proved impossible.

But the South Saskatchewan Regiment had done as much or more than could have been expected of them. With unfaltering courage, fighting always against the clock, they had put in attack after attack against the strongly fortified position of Quatre Vents Farm under the personal leadership of Lt.-Colonel Merritt and Major McTavish. As a result of individual acts of courage the pill-boxes of the outer defences had been taken by assault, but the farm held out.

Pourville village was well taken and strongly held on a perimeter, of necessity, too close for ultimate comfort. But the heights to the East and West of Pourville had defied the slender resources in men that could be spared against them, and had withstood with no great difficulty the bombardment from the sea of H.M.S. *Albrighton* and the Motor Gun Boat 317. Both these ships had given fine support within the pitiful limitations of their weapons, but the task of silencing light anti-aircraft batteries and anti-tank guns, well sited and concealed, and of continuously attacking the innumerable heavy machine-gun posts with decisive effect was beyond their power. In addition the enemy continued to bring up great numbers of horse-drawn mortars not only to drench the foreshore and approaches in a most murderous pattern of fire, but also to harass the troops fighting further inland. These weapons consistently outranged the best mortars available to our own troops by as much as seven hundred yards.

By nine o'clock perhaps a score of heavy machine-gun posts

and some light A/A guns had been put out of action mainly by accurate gunfire from the sea. In La Maison Blanche above the cliffs a platoon of the South Saskatchewan Regiment still held their own and neutralized a considerable weight of enemy fire while nourished at their posts on wine and cakes served by the French girls who had been the servants of the German officers.

Yet despite these successes the weight of enemy fire on Green Beach and its approaches had greatly increased, and with every minute, as the ebbing tide lengthened the foreshore below the shingle to lay bare the slippery seaweed-covered rocks and the sand under the shallows, the prospects for the withdrawal grew more ominous. At nine o'clock the assault landing craft, carrying Commander McClintock with his urgent message to hold the beach open, had been driven off by a concentration of gunfire that it would have been sheer suicide to attempt to defy. From the sea it seemed impossible that men still survived within those narrow confines, obscured in smoke and echoing incessantly to the crash of guns and the blast of the mortar bursts.

Nevertheless Lt.-Commander Prior, Lt. Miller, and the Medical Officer, Capt. F. W. Hayter, had found some shelter for the growing numbers of the wounded, and had not ceased their attentions at the constant risk of their lives. Their great worry at that time was their inability to send or to receive messages owing to the failure of the Beachmaster and signal party to get ashore from the motor gun boat. It was not until nearly ten o'clock that they knew that the withdrawal must be delayed for one hour to fit in with the new plans. By that time the idea that those marooned on Red and White Beaches might find an outlet through Pourville had been abandoned. It was, at any rate, quite hopeless.

At nine o'clock the South Saskatchewan Regiment, maintaining their assaults against Quatre Vents Farm with undiminished energy, and attempting to gain a foothold on the high ground on their flanks, still cherished the illusion that they had but one hour left to fight. For the rest, the failure of the Royal Hamilton Light Infantry and the tanks to put in an appearance told its own story, while the beat and thunder of the Dieppe guns backed by the Rommel, Goering and Hitler batteries added their sombre music to the dismal theme.

There was no other course open to the South Sasks but to hold on, and to batter away against the defences of the farm to shield the Queen's Own Cameron Highlanders on their withdrawal. And to the last they must hold Pourville with as much space as possible. At nine o'clock even ten o'clock began to seem a long way off.

For the Queen's Own Cameron Highlanders the realization of the march of events was less clear. The failure of the tanks to arrive had made it impossible for them to gain their objectives, but it did not carry with it a sinister message. And they were hard pressed; too hard pressed as time went by to have ears for anything but the gunfire directed against them. Vulnerable, with nearly two and a half miles of difficult country between them and the sea, and with every yard of it covered by mortars or snipers or both, they held on hoping to the last moment that reinforcements might come, and that in their rear Quatre Vents Farm might fall.

At half past nine o'clock, half an hour before they were due to begin to re-embark under their original and only known orders, the Camerons began to fight their way out to Pourville, carrying their wounded.

With the support platoon leading, with A Company shielding their flank, and C Company forming the rearguard, the battalion moved swiftly to gain the cover of Bernonville wood. They were under heavy fire from high ground in the region of Le Plessis.

Fighting every inch of the way, and hemmed in by enemy small-arms fire and mortars, the Camerons held steady with a discipline that could not have been surpassed. It was as though they fought an invisible foe while they themselves were in full view. But they gained Bernonville wood, and soon afterwards, as they came under heavy mortar fire on their right flank from the defenders of Quatre Vents Farm, they were sustained by the presence of the South Sasks fighting strongly to maintain pressure against the farm, and compelling the enemy to face both ways. Indeed, given a further half hour and Quatre Vents Farm might have fallen.

At four minutes to ten o'clock, four minutes ahead of time, the Camerons reached the outskirts of Pourville village to meet a platoon of the South Sasks and to learn that there was yet one full hour to run. The message had got through finally to Lt.-Commander Prior on the beach. The first landing craft would put in—or attempt to put in—at eleven o'clock.

The idea of holding the beach open had been abandoned.

In any case, it was impossible.

It was known that those fighting on the Red and White Beaches of Dieppe must be withdrawn from those beaches under the guns of the East and West headlands, and all the massed fire-power of mortars and field-guns the enemy could bring to bear. And that would not be all. The enemy had been stirred to action far beyond the Headquarters of 302 Division or 81 Corps and their local resources. At twenty minutes to ten o'clock Field Marshal von Runstedt, Commander-in-Chief in the West, committed the 10th Panzer Division to the battle. Mocked by the French civilians as they passed through Abbeville the enemy armour was advancing rapidly on Dieppe while reinforcements of infantry were entrained. A true appreciation of the situation could not have set such forces in motion. The Germans were frightened. In the air, too, they had begun to answer the challenge of the R.A.F., and the bombers were moving South from Holland and from Beauvais, while at this hour of ten o'clock at least two hundred fighters were joined in combat above the beaches and the sea.

2

At ten o'clock in Pourville village Lt.-Colonel Merritt and Major Law, commanding the Camerons, held hurried Council of War and set up a combined Headquarters in the Grand Central Hotel. Their two battalions had to stand and fight for a full hour against rapidly increasing enemy numbers, and with their only line of retreat enfiladed by innumerable enemy guns. In such circumstances a single hour is all eternity.

There was little room to manœuvre. The South Saskatchewan Regiment had not given back any of the ground gained throughout the morning, and it was vital now that not a yard should be given; for more was needed.

While in the centre the main body of the two battalions turned at bay upon the enemy that had pressed upon their heels, and with fierce counter attacks gained some elbow room round Pourville, the reserve company of the Camerons attempted to gain a foothold on the dangerous high ground to the West, and one company of the South Sasks held on grimly to a section of the high ground to the East.

From the outset it was clear that this would be a desperate fight against the clock. Without fire-power these men were at the mercy of enemy shelling and mortaring against which they could do nothing but hold fast, and defy the enemy to show themselves.

Meanwhile the stretcher bearers of the R.C.A.M.C. filtered the wounded down the narrow funnel of the line of retreat to the beach. Without pause for five hours Lt.-Commander Prior, Lt. Miller, and Capt. F. W. Hayter, wounded now himself, had worked on that battered and deadly shore to bring hope and comfort to men in grievous pain. These three men knew the worst. They saw the course that must be run steadily drawing out before their eyes, over the sands and the shallows that masked the ultimate truth of distance.

There was not long to wait. Before half past ten o'clock the first landing craft were closing the beach to bring off the wounded under all the covering fire that could be mustered.

The destroyer H.M.S. *Brocklesby* had now added her guns to the support fire as the stretcher bearers began the exodus of the wounded over two hundred yards of open ground. Hayter, Prior and Miller played their parts in that slow procession, matching their stride to the halting gait of crippled men, struggling on, unhurried, incapable of hurry, their arms about the necks of their helpers, while the water spouted in fierce jets to the lash of bullets in the shallows. It seemed then that there was a quiet core of peace in this slow ritual, as it might have been in the heart of the 'burning fiery furnace'. But these men, yielding themselves to this last chance, were not immune. As the searing fragments of the bursting mortar bombs tore into their flesh, many crumpled to lie still, while others, Prior and Miller among them, shuddered to the impact of their wounds and struggled on with their burdens, discovering somehow the strength to drag themselves again to the beach, for their work was not yet done.

There were few men unwounded in that long ordeal to gain the landing craft, waiting steadfastly under heavy fire as near in as they could float.

In and around Pourville the troops were still holding, but the enemy were inexorably closing in. The Camerons had been forced off the West heights, and the South Sasks could not cling to their small holding to the East. The enemy now dominated the beach and the slopes East of Pourville, forcing the withdrawal under direct fire over two hundred yards of open ground and one hundred and fifty yards of shallows.

It was fifteen minutes to eleven o'clock when the main force of landing craft began to come in, and the first troops braced themselves for that fateful journey.

Behind them the rearguard led by Lt.-Colonel Merritt faced the enemy, selling every yard of ground at a high price.

3

Throughout all these hours the deeds of men ashore were matched by the dogged determination of those afloat. Time after time the crews of the landing craft had closed the deadly beaches, intent upon their work of rescue, and seeming almost defenceless under the fire of the enemy guns as they plucked men from death, and gathered their grim harvest on the rim of the sea.

The crews of the landing craft had suffered heavily in killed and wounded. As lieutenants and petty officers had fallen their places had been filled at once by those nearest at hand; signalmen, ratings, even troopers and private soldiers found themselves at the helms of little ships, and at times in sole command. In that long-drawn-out relay, of which the last lap was about to be run, willing hands had been ready to grasp the batons as they fell.

Now, as the landing craft began to close Green Beach, sailing out of the smoke and haze that overlaid the sea, a supreme effort of fortitude was demanded and given. At sea the guns of H.M.S. *Brocklesby*, joined for a vital half hour by those of H.M.S. *Calpe* off the western end of Pourville beach, and of all the gun boats and support craft that could be spared, battered the machine-gun posts and mortar positions on the west heights overlooking Pourville. These ships, firing with fury and accuracy, for a time almost neutralized that massive source of enemy fire-power, but more they could not do.

On shore, joining themselves to this last supreme effort, the rearguard troops, inspired by the energy and courage of Lt.-Colonel Merritt and his few remaining officers, fought with redoubled strength and passion that their comrades might survive. While the rearguard held Pourville village, platoon followed platoon in good order to give close covering fire to their mates to gain the landing craft. There was at that time only one three-inch mortar left to the South Sasks, and with this their solitary piece of 'ordnance' they hurled bombs against the enemy, while with the two-inch mortar smoke was laid with some success over the deadly approaches to the sea.

The beach and foreshore of Pourville wore then the aspect of some nether region in which men moved like fearful shadows in the drifting smoke. The sky was grey with cloud. The sea was grey. The very air seemed grey; and through this limbo men moved in grisly procession, seeming wrapped in an appalling loneliness.

Over the shingle, over the weed wet rocks and the sand, and into the shallows, the first of the Camerons and the South Sasks struggled outwards towards the battered landing craft, and many splashed to their deaths to stain the salt shallows with their life's blood.

It seemed at first that this last sacrifice must be in vain, that men merely exchanged death on land for death in the water, and that there could be little hope. Men crumpled to their deaths as their hands reached out to grasp the walls of the little ships. Others died as they clambered on board. A direct hit caved in the bows of an assault craft to topple a cluster of men slowly back into the sea, there to flounder and to be mercilessly shot down.

It was a miracle that many got through to safety, yet by half past eleven o'clock five landing craft and one tank landing craft had rescued full cargoes from the shallows and cleared the beach under the guns of the *Brocklesby* and *Calpe*. All these owed their lives in no small measure to those still fighting valiantly to give them cover, to hold Pourville, and harass the strong enemy gun positions on the East hill.

In the last half hour Lt.-Colonel Merritt had inspired the men to great heights of courage, seeming himself to be everywhere in the battle. At one moment he was seen to lead a small body of men with Major D. C. Orme to silence some machine-guns on the cliffs towards the West of the beach. A few minutes later he was in the narrow approaches to the foreshore urging on his men to the boats, and giving covering fire. Again he was back in Pourville with the rearguard.

The last stand in Pourville had created great excitement among the French inhabitants. They had welcomed the arrival of the British almost as liberators, and from the first not only the young, but the middle-aged, had rushed to welcome the troops, and begging to be saved. Many had small bundles of their possessions and clamoured to join the Free French. But this had been forbidden. By half past eleven it had become impossible.

It was becoming clear with each minute, as the troops dwindled away and the guns of the East hill raked Pourville with deadly effect, that the hopes of saving the rearguard were disappearing fast. Two landing craft had transhipped their survivors to *Calpe*, and returned to try again. Other landing craft were still striving to close the beach, and a trickle of men fought their way out.

On the beach itself Lt.-Commander Prior and Lt. Miller refused to leave until the last, inspiring all with their calm and resolute air, and maintaining tenuous contact with Battalion Headquarters still holding out in the Grand Central Hotel. While Pourville held, many men might yet be saved, but there was an obvious dilemma: if the rearguard gave way the enemy flood would burst through. They must hold the door to the end. They could not hold it for themselves.

In the attack on the machine-gun posts Lt.-Colonel Merritt had at last been wounded. Waiting only for a rough field-dressing he dashed off once more towards Pourville. And this was the last seen of him, running alone towards the enemy and grasping up a Bren gun as he went. But it was not the last heard of him. In Pourville he rallied one hundred men to counter attack the enemy with such violence that they recoiled in spite of their overwhelming strength.

But time was fast running out. In a last effort to re-embark more troops from the beach, and to save the rearguard, Prior succeeded in getting a message through to the Colonel asking him to set fire to the houses. If that could be done the smoke might shield the rearguard in a bold dash for safety. Hastily collecting all incendiary grenades the Colonel set about this last task, but it was in vain. All the incendiary grenades were defective. The last chance had gone.

According to the official record, the rearguard would have been saved if it had been possible to shell the East hill. But the East hill was never silenced.

Not until all hope was gone did Lt.-Commander Prior leave the beach on which he had been among the first to set foot, and from which he had not budged through those long hours.

Meanwhile in Pourville Merritt and his men made their last stand, fighting on long after the last landing craft had left the shore of France for home, and until their last shot was fired. Helpless then, and near to exhaustion, hemmed in on all sides, they were captured. They did not surrender.

CHAPTER SEVENTEEN

DIEPPE: BEFORE THE WITHDRAWAL

I

THE whole problem of the withdrawal had been greatly simplified by the appalling losses suffered, and by the decision to abandon all material ashore. It had become a case of men only, and it was doubtful whether the most optimistic observer counted on saving more than half the total originally planned. This would also mean a great saving in time. Instead of a steady routine drawn out over more than three hours, an attempt must be made to scoop up as many men as possible in the shortest possible time.

The situation at sea was more satisfactory than could have been foreseen. The slight enemy naval threats reported had failed to materialize, and the great concourse of vessels had suffered much less interference than they had expected.

By ten o'clock the first of the German bombers had begun to arrive to add to the targets of the naval anti-aircraft gunners, and the fight overhead was moving steadily towards its climax to the obvious satisfaction of Air Marshal Leigh-Mallory and the R.A.F. In this department communications had worked with complete smoothness from the start, and Air Commodore Cole, observing the development of the air battle from the bridge of H.M.S. *Calpe*, had been able to keep his chief fully informed.

At precisely four minutes to ten o'clock, at that moment when the Camerons had reached Pourville to learn of the one-hour delay in their withdrawal, Air Commodore Cole signalled No.11 Group, Fighter Command:

'Situation too obscure to give useful report. Air co-operation faultless. Enemy air opposition increasing. Have you any questions?'

Eight minutes later Air Commodore Cole asked for smoke to be laid over Red and White Beaches from eleven o'clock for one half hour. The first of the enemy bombers was then crashing into the sea. Meanwhile the simplified withdrawal plan was going ahead swiftly under the direction of Commander McClintock. The little ships were easily assembled from the Boat Pool, and took their stations with the assault and motor landing craft leading, and with all available tank landing craft formed up in the rear and ready to move into their positions one mile offshore.

All this was done under cover of continuous smoke-screens, and under the necessity to manœuvre constantly to avoid the attacks of enemy fighters, bombers, and the shelling of the coastal batteries. These batteries resisted all the efforts of the R.A.F. and constituted the greatest threat to the Naval Force.

At twenty minutes past ten o'clock, with the small craft ready to move, the order was given to the destroyers to form their line to follow them in. Every craft that could be spared from the essential patrolling of the flanks had been collected for the final effort.

Under the sea wall of Red Beach, suffering heavy casualties throughout the whole morning, the Essex Scottish Regiment waited anxiously on the defensive, nursing their dwindling ammunition against the moment of their going. At the western end of the beach Brigadier Southam maintained contact, and attempted to exercise command over the defence, and give coherence to the final effort at withdrawal.

Towards eleven o'clock every man then on the beach braced himself for the final effort, knowing well that he would need all his courage, yet determined to deny to the enemy the satisfaction of his living body. The conception of the withdrawal had always been bold: now it had taken on a quality of tragic heroism. But the long dim toll of the hours had been shot through with the vivid exploits of bold and resourceful men, revealing in their desperate forays the success so nearly within the grasp of the expedition. For once that hard defensive crust was burst open the enemy inner core was soft.

It had been estimated that the troops of the German garrison were of poor quality, and so it proved.

It is known that at least six small groups of men made effective raids through the town. There may have been more. At least two tanks fought on in the heart of Dieppe until their ammunition was exhausted, and of their fate nothing is known. But outstanding in the roll of these few are the exploits of Sergeant Dubuc of the Fusiliers Mont-Royal.

For an hour Dubuc and his one companion had fought the

stranded tank of Lt.-Colonel Andrews from its exposed position on the sand. As soon as the last shell had been fired Dubuc decided to make a dash for the sea wall. Two men might easily live where fifty would almost surely die. With his companion he reached a point under the sea wall close to the invisible boundary between Red and White Beaches. In that area the wounded Lt.-Colonel Ménard strove to hold together a nucleus of his regiment and to organize as much aggressive defensive fire as possible. He was still unaware of the fate of nearly half of his men. They had seemed to disappear, and no contact had been made. In Dubuc's mind was a very strong awareness of his Colonel's plight, and a burning desire to do something to redeem, in however small a fashion, the *débâcle* of the landing. He was fully aware, too, that his regiment had been sent to the relief of Red Beach.

It is impossible to measure such men as Dubuc by normal standards. It does not seem to have entered his head to sit down under the wall in a defensive role, and at once eleven men of the Fusiliers Mont-Royal rallied to his side. Well armed with tommy-guns, Brens and grenades, they followed their leader in swift bounds to cross the esplanade.

By this time a murky acrid pall of battle overlay the whole scene, the incessant gunfire, the smoke and flames of burning buildings, the smoke-screens laid continuously at sea and wafted inshore by the freshening wind from the West, all combined to make a twilit world of the broad boulevards and the gardens of the sea front.

The crossing of these wide open spaces presented no problem to Dubuc. Gaining the backyards of the hotels and boarding houses he pressed on with his men into the town, clearing the streets with bursts of Bren-gun fire, and reaching the Rue de Sygogne almost without incident. There Dubuc's party came up with Captain Vandeloe of their own regiment, marauding with a body of twenty men in high fettle, having found themselves more than a match for all the enemy they had encountered.

Captain Vandeloe had attacked in the rear the hotels and boarding houses with their fronts on the Boulevard de Verdun. Most of these buildings had been fortified as strong-points, and had added greatly to the direct fire-power of the enemy in the early stages. This much, at least, the withdrawal would be spared, for Vandeloe's party had winkled out the enemy with great effect.

They had also brought down most of the snipers from these roof-tops, and those few who remained were no longer able to concentrate with any sense of detachment upon their deadly work.

These successes had inspired Vandeloe, and he proposed to carry on clearing enemy out of houses and key points until it was time to go.

The meeting of these two, the Captain and the Sergeant, seems to have been brief and buoyant, and mutually inspiring.

Dubuc turned East. There lay the tasks he would find for himself, for it was not only in his mind to inflict as much damage upon the enemy as possible, but also to do this in the area to which his regiment had been committed. As for his men, they were eager to follow wherever he might lead. His personal magnetism was astounding, in keeping with the kind of character beloved of a Dumas or a Sabatini, and but seldom encountered outside the pages of romantic fiction. Dubuc led on swiftly towards the docks.

Approaching the dock area the small party were at once held up by machine-gun posts covering intersections and entrances, but not for long. Moving with great speed and determination round the flanks, and skilfully using covering fire, Dubuc succeeded in destroying the machine-gun posts with grenades used with great daring, and forced a way through to the edge of the *Bassin Duquesne*. Here they were still under intermittent machine-gun fire and sniping, and confronted by a seeming emptiness, bleak and desolate. It was as though they had burst through an outer wall from a world of din and known danger, to an unnatural silence, and a sense of being watched. There were few shots, but those few held a note of peculiar personal menace in the thin whine of their coming.

It would have been simple to have turned back, as men do confronted with a *cul-de-sac*, and for a moment Dubuc halted on this eerie edge of the dockland, waving his men to crouch in the shelter and shadow while he got his bearings. The *Bassin Duquesne* was empty. Skirting the *Bassin*, moving swiftly in sharp bounds, setting the tempo to those who followed, Dubuc pressed on. There was something indomitable about him, and even at this time an aura of seeming safety.

So they came quickly through to reach the *Bassin du Canada*, and to find there two of the invasion barges that had been ear-marked as the prey of the Navy. These were the prizes Dubuc sought. His party were still under intermittent fire, and it was vital to act swiftly before this fire gave warning to the barge crews. A sense of exhilaration seems to have uplifted these few men at this moment: it may have been that their French blood gave them a sense of 'belonging', of being native against the alien Nazi. They followed Dubuc as stealthily as cats, to swoop silently and suddenly upon the barges, and to overwhelm the crews in brief and fierce hand to hand fighting. In five minutes Dubuc had won the barges, and it would not have been beyond his imagination to have attempted to sail them out to sea. That task would have been impossible.

Leaving the barges with their dead, Dubuc then turned South on the railway tracks with the idea that his party might in some way hold up enemy reinforcements. This was unwise. Well armed, keeping the initiative, it was credible and even probable that Dubuc and his men might have overwhelmed three times their numbers, but they were now out of grenades, and their ammunition was almost used up.

For about one thousand yards, divided into two groups, one on either side of the tracks, taking what cover they could find, Dubuc and his men moved forward apparently unseen. It was by that time nearing half past ten o'clock. Little time remained, and strong enemy patrols were already moving in Dieppe in the vanguard of reinforcements.

It was in Dubuc's mind to give up this barren course, and move off into the town, when he came suddenly under heavy fire from an enemy patrol. It was impossible to get away. The small party with one mind stood their ground, and fought to the last round. In five minutes it was all over, and Dubuc surrendered. That in itself was a delicate operation, for it is sometimes easier to be killed than to be captured in such circumstances.

At that moment Dubuc appeared to be overcome with exhaustion, and utterly disconsolate. The stuffing seemed to have been knocked right out of him, but the Germans were not disposed to take any chances. Not content with disarming their captives they took the unusual precaution of forcing them to strip down to their underclothes, but they left them their boots. In that sorry state the prisoners were lined up with their faces to a wall near a siding, and left under guard. At a command from the guard they kept their arms above their heads. They were helpless, and to most men, however brave, it must have seemed that the game was up. But Dubuc was acutely alert, his ears tuned to the diminishing beat of boots as the patrol moved on, and sensitive to new sounds.

There could be but a few minutes in which to act—if it were possible to act at all. Dubuc's head had slumped down to his shoulder. He stood in an attitude of dejection, and from that position he was able to watch the guard. The man stood with his rifle at the ready, alert, half turned to keep his prisoners in view while also watching the lines of approach. In postures of weariness and despair his prisoners appeared to need the support of the wall. Dubuc himself was breathing heavily.

Two or three minutes went by in a silence broken only by the harsh small sounds of men in distress, and the pattern of gunfire that seemed almost to come from another world.

Dubuc had carefully revolved in his mind the chances of a break. He braced himself for action, determined somehow to lure the sentry within reach of his hands. Dubuc, of course, was completely unarmed, standing there, rather ridiculous at first glance in his Summer singlet and shorts, and with his heavy ammunition boots. He made a sound like a dry groan to gain the attention of the sentry. His hands above his head lay against the wall, as though but for that he must have fallen.

"Water!" he croaked. "Water!"

The guard took two steps towards him, and for an instant was off guard. In that instant Dubuc turned with the speed of a panther and smashed the man down with his bare hands, and killed him.

"Go!" he ordered. His voice was very quiet and gentle. "Back to the beach. Each man for himself."

Within a minute the twelve men had gone without trace, each man taking his way alone through the back streets of Dieppe, heading for the beach. If they were seen by the enemy, it may be that the strange sight of men running at full speed through the streets in singlets and shorts was strange enough to make reaction slow. In their various ways they reached the beach.

It was almost exactly eleven o'clock when Dubuc found his wounded Colonel, and reported, excusing himself for his un-military appearance. It was a moment of decision. The squadrons of the R.A.F. were swooping down exactly on time over the East headland laying the curtain of smoke that must be a shield to all these men in their hopes of escape. And out of that massive pall the enemy guns had begun to blaze fiercely at the invisible targets, too numerous and too confined to be missed. In an instant the whole foreshore became an inferno of smoke and sound and fury, and of men moving down over the stones.

Out of the sea smoke Dubuc could see the assault craft coming in through the shallows. It was no short passage now over a steep shingle bank, but a long and perilous journey. Without a word Sergeant Dubuc stooped to lift his wounded Colonel in his arms, and strode out towards the sea.

2

The arrival of the landing craft off the Red and White Beaches of Dieppe was not only the signal for which the survivors of the Essex Scottish and the Royal Hamilton Light Infantry had waited for so long, it was also the signal to the massed German mortars and field-guns to join themselves to the enfilade fire of the East and West headlands to take a final toll of the British troops. They would also take a heavy toll of the light craft and their naval crews, so vulnerable and steadfast under the guns.

If this were indeed invasion—the 'second front' for which the Russians, and even the British themselves, clamoured so harshly and insistently—it was decisively repulsed. If it were not, then severe losses of landing craft must burden the British in their future intentions.

Perhaps never before—and never since—have so many light vessels, many of them unarmoured and so hopelessly out-gunned, submitted themselves, protected mainly by smoke-screens, for more than an hour to almost point-blank bombardment from so great an array of guns.

Many of the anti-tank and light anti-aircraft guns that had roared a murderous welcome in the dawn had been silenced, and especially had the armament of the West headland suffered, but the heavy mortars and field-guns brought up by the enemy more than balanced the loss. The pattern of fire had changed, but not for the better. Had the Royal Air Force failed to provide full cover, and to meet the massive challenge they had at last provoked, it seems certain that this story must have ended in complete disaster. As it was, the German fighters and bombers were rendered almost powerless to interfere in any battle but their own.

On that beach that had become a tormented wasteland, a chaos of shattered stones, and tangled wire hung with the limp bodies of the dead, and shrouded in fumes and smoke, the living rose like ghosts from the cramped positions in which they had survived withering gun and mortar fire for nearly six hours, and mindful of their wounded comrades, many of them matching their paces to the slowest, they made their way towards the landing craft.

The remnants of the Essex Scottish, deprived of their Colonel, wounded and finally captured in his efforts to lead his men beyond the wall, had preserved many of their smoke canisters for the last service of masking their withdrawal. These they now hurled over the esplanade wall and, gathering their wounded, tottered out into the open to face more than two hundred yards of shore and shallows stippled with the deadly bursts of high explosive. The curve of the beach gave them the shortest distance of any on this mile-long shore, but it was far enough. Ahead of them the crews of the landing craft waited, saved only from almost certain death by the drifting curtains of smoke, and the concentrated support fire that had been organized for this last hour.

But on White Beach there were scenes of more violent action as the Royal Hamiltons began to fight their way out with the prisoners they had taken in the Casino. For more than three hours elements of the Royal Hamiltons, the Sappers, and a small body of the Fusiliers Mont-Royal under Sergeant-Major Dumais, had held the strongly fortified Casino building against repeated enemy attacks. At the same time they had provided something of a base for the marauding bands of Royal Hamiltons and Sappers and a focal point on which to retreat.

Sergeant Hickson, who had broken out under the covering fire of the tank as soon as he had made his contribution to the capture of the building in the early morning, had fared well. Apart from the considerable destruction he and his men had achieved, they had also engaged and wiped out a strong patrol of the enemy at the intersection of Rue de la Martinière, Rue de l'Hôtel de Ville, and Rue de la Halle au Blé, North of St. Remy Church. Following that action, and hampered by snipers directed by civilians wearing arm-bands, they had attacked the enemy in house after house with success.

The civilians, as it turned out, were enemy agents, and Hickson had only let himself be fooled once, and for a moment. There is no doubt that the French inhabitants of Dieppe were loyal to the British cause, which was, of course, their own. They remained indoors.

Finally Sergeant Hickson had withdrawn his party under growing enemy pressure and regained the Casino. It was then nearing the hour of withdrawal, and the Casino had to be held to the last, not only to deny its use to the enemy, but also to give some covering fire for the withdrawal from that quarter of the beach.

While Sergeant Hickson had been fighting his battles, Capt. Hill with C.S.M. Stewart and their party had also enjoyed some success after gaining the shelter of the cinema, and avoiding the road block at the corner of the Boulevard de Verdun. Using the cinema as a base they had made three sorties to attack enemy patrols, inflicting heavy casualties without loss to themselves. They had then held the cinema for two hours against repeated attacks, until they had judged it necessary to fight their way back to the cover of the Casino.

At the last, therefore, the Casino building was strongly held. Its defences had been strengthened by the Germans within the last few weeks, and the slit trenches the Germans had provided for all-round defence were well manned. On the second floor Sergeant-Major Dumais and his small group had managed to maintain aggressive fire for three hours.

All through the morning the garrison of the Casino and the 'fighting patrols' basing themselves upon it had waged direct warfare in contact with enemy troops. Now, as the landing craft approached the shore, these few prepared to disengage.

Major Lazier and Capt. Currie had been among the first to enter the Casino, and these two officers had done much to give coherence to the defence throughout the morning. They now covered the withdrawal with rifle fire, and fighting all the way they began an orderly retreat towards the far and faint promise of safety. They faced a course longer by at least one hundred and fifty yards than that to be traversed by the badly mauled Essex Scottish in the East, but their morale was high.

At six minutes past eleven o'clock the first survivors of the Red and White Beaches reached the landing craft, and it was twenty minutes past twelve o'clock when the last vessel cleared that tragic shore. In that hour and a quarter the naval crews snatched one thousand men from death or servitude, and paid a high price in their own blood.

CHAPTER EIGHTEEN

VANQUISH

I

FROM the moment that Commander McClintock had given the
order to set 'Operation Vanquish' in motion the naval crews had
geared themselves to meet the hour of crisis with a supreme effort.
At nine o'clock it was already difficult to the point of foolhardiness
to attempt to close the main beaches. By eleven o'clock they would
have to accomplish the impossible. Most of the crews of the
landing craft had been in and out since dawn, picking men out of
the sea, and rescuing the wounded. They knew all about it. And
there was no possibility of improvement, but simply the certainty
that with every hour the enemy would be able to concentrate
more power upon these narrow shores, and remain out of reach
of the naval guns. The change from that terrific close fire of the
first landing was not for the better.

In a curious way it gave them confidence. By the time they
might hope to steer for England they would have spent at least
nine hours in the enemy's backyard, a horde of little ships with
gun boats, motor launches, a sloop and eight destroyers. It was
beginning to appeal to their sense of humour. The rumours of
approaching E-boats had proved false. Their aircraft, fighting
overhead since before the dawn with seventy miles of sea and a
lot of dangerous sky between them and their bases, had the beating
of the enemy flying over his own guns, and with his airfields
under his wings. They were almost glad that they hadn't a battleship out there to smash the coastal batteries to hell and pulverize
the headlands, and throughout the two hours of intense preparation
a strong sense of defiance pervaded the crews of the little ships.
The enemy was afraid of them, and they knew it. The biggest
thing they had was a Hunt class destroyer—not even a light
cruiser! It was the kind of situation this war constantly produced
for them, and it was the kind of challenge they faced the best.

Nevertheless few had set sail with any realization of the lack
of fire-power. They had gone in to land with high hearts. They

had suffered heavy casualties. They had high hearts still; but no illusions. They were out-gunned to the point where they thought it was 'typical'. The knowledge that they were within easy range of at least three shore batteries and the artillery of an Army Corps, with all the advantages of the stability of the land to fire from, added a spice almost of madness to the task ahead. But they thanked God for the R.A.F., for if they failed they had no doubt that the German guns would blow them out of the water.

No man in all that fleet had cause to doubt the courage and endurance of the R.A.F.—much had happened since Dunkirk—but it seemed certain that the pilots of the Hurricanes and Spitfires, flying sortie after sortie out of England since before the dawn, had a tremendous struggle on their hands.

Long before eleven o'clock the enemy heavy bombers were droning high overhead, and the naval A/A gunners were kept busy, blazing away with Oerlikons whenever the enemy fighters dived down out of the murk with their machine-guns blazing. Already the wreckage of a dozen aircraft was strewn over the sea, some of them our own, and there was a sense in every man that the battle was moving to its climax.

It was in such circumstances, manœuvring under cover of continuous smoke, that the ships made ready to close the main beaches for the last time. The tide had ebbed to the full, and they cursed the shallows that would force exhausted men to wade out under a murderous barrage of high explosive. Every bit of available fire-power had been carefully organized to give them cover. Details of the Toronto Scottish were manning four tank landing craft with forty-eight machine-guns on anti-aircraft mountings. They would make it hot for any low-level attempts at bombing or strafing the landing craft.

And so the small craft, many of them without armour, went steadily in to close the beaches while the destroyers and gun boats and every craft with a gun blazed away with all they had. They knew that they were making a lot of noise and little fury, but it was comforting all the same, comforting also to the men on the beaches.

All that foreshore had become a No-Man's-Land, a between world of smoke and shadows and blistering shell fire. Dieppe itself was invisible. All that could be seen from the landing craft were men straggling out through the smoke in the midst of a creeping barrage, and from that moment the shallows of the sea seemed to become a series of small enclosed worlds, in which each landing craft and those who strove to reach it was peculiarly alone.

There was no wild rush, no surge of desperate men threatening to overwhelm their rescuers, but simply a slow procession. Out from the long beach the shadowy figures came, bearing their wounded, stumbling stoically through the water, hands at last outstretched to hands dragging them on board.

There was very little tracer now; very little direct fire from machine-guns and small arms, but the barrage was thickening up to a murderous intensity far more deadly than the point-blank greeting of the dawn.

The smoke curtains that veiled the headlands had at once warned the enemy of renewed activity, and he was quick to respond, as yet uncertain of the British intention. Indeed, it seems more likely from the enemy's deeds, rather than his words, that he expected heavier landings, and did not at that time suspect an attempt at withdrawal. The fear of invasion was deep, and large forces on land and in the air had been set in motion towards Dieppe. These were out of proportion to the size of the raid.

While the intense bombing attacks went in against the head-lands and the coastal batteries, the massed field-guns and heavy mortars of the German 81 Corps found the range, and brought down a tremendous barrage upon the landing craft and the fore-shore. It seemed a miracle that men or craft could survive. Many craft capsized and sank as they strove to clear the shore. Men clung on where they could, even grasping ropes to be towed through the water until their strength failed, or willing hands came to their aid. Here and there groups of men struggled in the water. Motor launches and gun boats grappled overloaded and sinking vessels, and transhipped their living cargoes, while others rushed at speed to the rescue of the drowning. Assault craft, already overburdened and badly holed, picked more survivors out of the water, unable to deny a chance to any man.

Yet, miraculously the tank landing craft waiting one mile offshore were filled, and the battered landing craft with their smitten crews returned again and again to the beaches for more.

Through the eyes of one or two individual survivors it is possible to get an authentic glimpse of some aspects of that brave struggle on the edge of the sea. One said:

"I made my way out to an L.C.A.,[1] but the first one I came to was hit and I was knocked off. I was picked up by another which was overcrowded and sinking, but another craft came alongside and took off most of the men, leaving the rest of us to bale out until we attracted the attention of a further ship, which stopped and took us on board."

Another said:

"We got back to the beach and out to an L.C.A. Before I got in it pulled out, and I hung on to some ropes and was pulled along. A bullet hit me in the arm and knocked me off the rope, but I managed to grab the iron bars by the propeller, and after it pulled me a long way a couple of people pulled me up over the back, and that L.C.A. brought me to Newhaven."

Yet in that shambles there were men whose strength and steadiness, both on shore and in the little ships, seemed to gain for them a special providence. Among these was Sergeant Dubuc striding out from Red Beach with his wounded Colonel in his arms as calmly as though he were on holiday. The Sergeant put his Colonel on board a large landing craft and did not move until he had seen it safely clear of the shallows. Then he returned again to Red Beach, and when next he made the journey from the shore he carried a wounded N.C.O. of the Essex Scottish, and this man, too, he saw safely away. Not until he had saved all he could did Sergeant Dubuc save himself, boarding an assault craft and transhipping to a tank landing craft as though on a routine exercise.

Here and there along that mile of deadly foreshore there were others of the quality of Sergeant Dubuc, quietly aiding wounded, and saving the withdrawal from the confusion that was always within a hairsbreadth. On the beach itself Brigadier Southam ordered the withdrawal with unfaltering calm, maintaining contact with the Military Force Commander on board *Calpe*. It was clear that Brigadier Southam conceived his place to be with his men to the last.

Meanwhile the retreat from White Beach went ahead steadily

[1] Assault Landing Craft.

under bold leadership. In the fighting retreat from the Casino Sergeant-Major Dumais had been prominent, and had finally embarked his men safely, returning himself to the beach for wounded. Then at the last the Sergeant-Major, struggling out with a wounded man, just managed to get his burden on board as the assault craft, overloaded and badly holed, dragged away to sea, leaving Dumais alone in the shallows.

It was then within a minute or two of noon. The smoke was clearing from the headlands and the beaches. It had saved the naval crews from something like a massacre, and they had faced their task throughout with astounding fortitude. But now it was becoming suicidal to attempt to close the beaches. A terrific air battle had developed, straining the pilots of the R.A.F. to the uttermost limits of their endurance as the entire German Air Force in the West was steadily committed to the battle. Tactical reconnaissance aircraft, returning from sorties far inland, flew low over the Headquarters ships H.M.S. *Calpe* and H.M.S. *Fernie* to make certain that their messages should be heard. The Germans were on the move. The end was near.

Throughout that long last hour *Calpe* gave leadership of the highest order, and was a constant inspiration. At half past eleven o'clock, having observed and aided in the relief of Green Beach and picked up two boatloads of survivors, the *Calpe* had turned east in an attempt to close Red Beach. Every available space on board was by then crammed with wounded, but she continued to inspire the work of rescue with great daring. Under her direction the motor launches were rounding up all possible landing craft to send them in again and again.

All through that hour Commander McClintock had survived in the forefront, keeping contact with the rescuing vessels and the Headquarters ship, and gauging the narrow margin between suicide and hope. By noon he thought that the naval crews had saved close on one thousand men. Still the Commander hung on. He knew that many still lived on that beach of stones, including Brigadier Southam, and every man was prepared to try and try again while trying could snatch a single life from that waste land of splintering steel.

At noon, under the orders of *Calpe*, the Motor Launch 194 made an attempt to collect a few more landing craft, and to go in again. They could not close the beach. But it had become impossible now for men to attempt the journey outward from the cover of the wall. The element of chance had gone.

At twenty minutes past twelve o'clock, convinced that further efforts were useless, Commander McClintock signalled:

'No more evacuation possible.'

On board *Calpe* Major-General Roberts confronted Capt. Hughes-Hallett, asking for a further effort. The idea of leaving the beaches while any man remained alive revolted every man afloat. It was a situation of pure anguish. In a few hours two brigades of the 2nd Canadian Infantry Division had been smashed, together with the loss of almost all their senior officers. To the Military Force Commander it was a calamity, and he could not bring himself to go. The words possible and impossible in the end must bear their true meanings. The impossible had already been achieved. Reluctantly Capt. Hughes-Hallett signalled to Commander McClintock:

'If no further evacuation possible, withdraw.'

This signal was reported to Commander McClintock without the 'If', and he at once brought the evacuation to an end. There was indeed no room for 'if'.

Realizing themselves lost, those men of the Fusiliers Mont-Royal who had been trapped under the West headland since the moment of landing, and had survived in great danger and discomfort while entirely impotent, surrendered to the enemy. They had been without orders and without means of communication since landing. Some very few had got away, probably to their deaths. At the last, two hundred and eighty-eight officers and men, one hundred of them wounded, gave themselves up.

2

As soon as the order had been given to bring the evacuation to an end the whole fleet began the process of assembly four miles seaward of Dieppe. The Navy had focused almost its entire effort towards the land while taking the minimum precautions for its own safety. But now, as the ships turned to face the voyage home, their own battle became paramount.

Few knew, or had time to know, the extent of the furious combat that raged overhead, or that for more than two hours the R.A.F. had thwarted all the attempts of the enemy bombers to bomb the landing craft. The naval A/A gunners had been kept busy defending their craft from the diving attacks of enemy fighters, but without the Spitfires and Hurricanes they would have been overwhelmed.

While the little ships drew away from the land led by H.M.S. *Fernie*, the destroyers, manœuvring at speed behind smoke-screens, continued their bombardment of the coast.

Even then Capt. Hughes-Hallett was reluctant to turn his back on Dieppe. Brigadier Southam still maintained contact with Major-General Roberts. Under the sea wall elements of the Royal Hamiltons were still fighting. In Pourville Lt.-Colonel Merritt was making his last brave stand at the head of the last one hundred men. And by the roadside, within one hundred yards of the Rommel battery behind Blue Beach, Lt.-Colonel Catto still lay in the ditch with his handful of men, not without hope.

At ten minutes to one o'clock the Naval Force Commander decided to make an attempt to close the main beaches with his ship, and to see for himself beyond a shadow of doubt. With the Assault Landing Craft 155 and 188 on either bow, *Calpe* steered for the eastern end of Red Beach under the menace of the Bismarck headland.

Calpe came out of the cover of smoke like an avenger, engaging the machine-gun posts on the harbour breakwater, as though at the last to fight a personal battle with the enemy. It was a challenge swiftly answered. Nine cable lengths offshore the destroyer came under heavy fire, but the Naval Force Commander was resolved to know the worst with his own eyes, and with all the guns she could bring to bear in action the ship, manœuvring brilliantly under the hands of Commander J. H. Wallace on the bridge, steamed broadside on to that long beach.

It seemed to the watchers on the *Calpe* as though some elemental violence had laid waste that whole expanse in some tortured upheaval, piling up stones, scooping out deep hollows, and over all the grotesque litter of a battlefield, the derelict craft and tanks, the pitiful shapes of death, limp on the stones, on the sand, and floating in the shallow water.

Reluctantly *Calpe* turned away into the cover of the smoke-screens. Capt. Hughes-Hallett was convinced that no more could be done, yet he continued to seek ways to do more. But soon after one o'clock, just as the Naval Force Commander was considering sending in the shallower draught gun boat *Locust* for one last effort, Major-General Roberts received a message from Brigadier Southam, signalling the end.

The remaining troops were surrendering. Enemy reinforcements were detraining at Dieppe railway station.

At eight minutes past one o'clock Brigadier Southam was forced to give up. He had directed the battle first from the beach, later from the Casino, maintaining contact from first to last.

3

Immediately upon receiving the last signal from the beach *Calpe*, with her accompanying vessels, turned away from the French coast to join the convoy of nearly two hundred ships already setting out through the mine-swept channels for England. The destroyers *Brocklesby*, *Bleasdale*, *Berkeley*, *Albrighton* and *Slazak*, together with the gun boat *Locust*, supporting the troops ashore until the end, hastened now to join *Fernie* and the gun boats in defence of the convoy. The weather was worsening. Under the low cloud the heavy smoke hung like a pall, and it was the sky now that demanded attention.

At about that time, within a minute or two of a quarter past one o'clock, a JU. 88, hard pressed by fighters of the R.A.F., jettisoned a heavy bomb in a vain attempt to escape destruction, and sank the destroyer *Berkeley* with this single chance blow. The bomb struck slightly forward of amidships, destroying the bridge and wrecking the wardroom. The boiler-room and engine-room were at once flooded, and *Berkeley* broke her back.

Wing Commander S. H. Skinner, R.A.F. Observer of Combined Operations Headquarters, had been standing on the bridge at the side of Lt. I. J. S. Yorke, R.N., in command of *Berkeley*. Both were killed. A third man, Lt.-Colonel L. B. Hillsinger, of the U.S. Army Air Corps, was blown off the bridge to the forward deck, where he sat staring in anger and consternation at the place where his right foot had been. The foot, with the shoe still on it, could be seen floating a few yards from the sinking destroyer.

The vessel was at that moment alive with furious activity, with sailors running to aid the wounded and to the rescue of others who were trapped below. Two sailors came at once to the aid of the American Colonel, and his behaviour impressed itself deeply upon them, even in their urgency. The Colonel continued to sit up, staring alternately at his right stump and at his missing foot wearing the shoe. Suddenly with a gesture of intense irritation he tore the shoe from his good left foot and flung it after the other into the water.

"Take the goddam pair!"

The Colonel turned then to the sailors.

"New shoes," he said. "Bought them this week. First time on. What d'you know!" He seemed unaware of pain.

One of the steam gun boats had at once come to the rescue, and was swiftly alongside the sinking destroyer, while *Albrighton* stood by. There was little time to lose, and the last of the wounded were transhipped within ten minutes.

By that time surgical dressings were getting scarce, but the naval medical personnel helped by R.C.A.M.C. did their best to make the wounded comfortable. Lt.-Colonel Hillsinger declined all but the treatment necessary to save his life. He refused injections. He refused a bunk, and insisted on lying out on the deck of the gun boat looking up at the sky.

"I'm meant to be observing this air battle," he said. "The Wing Commander's dead." And he went on doing his job, and doing it well. In the words of the official record he continued to 'inspire all by his courageous bearing' throughout the remainder of that long day.

Fifteen minutes after this chance bomb, dropped blind, and not even at a venture, had done its unhappy work, H.M.S. *Albrighton* sank the Hunt class destroyer *Berkeley* by torpedo fire.

The air battle had now reached an intensity that was a growing threat to the vulnerable convoy, and as the destroyers steamed at speed, putting up a barrage to protect themselves and the wide array of ships that had now become the sole target of the enemy, fighters began to dive out of the low cloud to the attack. All that morning the enemy fighters and bombers had failed materially to molest the ships, and even the landing craft had been protected to the last by the great efforts of the Air Force. But this was the enemy's last chance. Strung out across the Channel, confined to the mine-swept channels, and with the weather steadily deteriorating, the little ships were more vulnerable than they had been at any time.

At half past one o'clock a fighter diving steeply out of cloud sprayed the bridge of *Calpe* with machine-gun fire, severely wounding Air Commodore Cole. He had maintained perfect contact with Combined Operations Headquarters until that moment, and made possible in large measure the wonderful air co-operation.

This was the hour of greatest danger from the air, and the various observers carried on His Majesty's ships were getting their fill of excitement. For most of them it had been a day of frustration. Commander E. B. Strauss of the United States Navy was on board *Calpe*. Brigadier-General Lucian K. Truscott, U.S. Army, and Colonel F. A. Hart, U.S. Marine Corps, were carried by *Fernie*. There was also a United States observer on board *Bleasdale*, but for him it was an unprofitable morning.

By this time it had become very dangerous for any ship to move away from the concentrated barrage, but while *Fernie* and the other destroyers steamed on steadily for home, *Calpe*, notwithstanding her full cargo of wounded, turned eastward to the rescue of an R.A.F. pilot reported down in the sea.

The Air-Sea Rescue launches were sailing in almost under the coastal guns in their efforts to rescue their pilots, and were suffering heavily. They needed all the help that could be spared.

Furious now for a prize, the German bombers picked out the lone destroyer, and in two dive-bombing attacks *Calpe* was badly shaken and damaged by near misses from which her crew sustained more casualties. It was nearly three o'clock when she returned to the convoy. The first of the little ships were by then through the western mine-swept channel and within sight of Newhaven.

Meanwhile in mid Channel and over the French coast the air battle raged with unabated fury, and the enemy had begun to send out single bombers to harry the ships from the cloud cover.

The R.A.F. had said that they would put up an umbrella over all this operation, and maintain it to the end against whatever force the enemy dared to bring against them. The R.A.F. made good their boast.

CHAPTER NINETEEN

THE AIR BATTLE

Two Spitfires of 129 Squadron diving in to machine-gun the Pointe d'Ailly light west of Varengeville at fifteen minutes to five o'clock fired the first shots in the Dieppe Raid. The Pointe d'Ailly light was the Observation Post for the Hess battery. Throughout the night it had flashed its normal characteristic, and had led, in that last hour, the Assault Craft of No. 4 Commando towards their goal, and the sight of the Spitfires going in to the attack cheered the men of Lord Lovat's Commando, tense in their landing craft, as they began to close the beaches.

Ten miles to the eastward the chance encounter of No. 5 Group with the German armed trawlers had not disturbed the enemy. Neither, it seems, did the attack on the Hess Observation Post. The Dieppe harbour light continued to flash, hoping to lead in a small convoy expected from the west. The enemy slept. Nothing appeared to disturb him. Yet this was a period of the highest alertness. Once a week since May practice alerts and exercises had been held.

From that zero minute of fifteen minutes to five o'clock the attacks of the R.A.F. developed exactly as planned to co-ordinate with the landings along those eleven miles of coast. By a quarter past five o'clock attacks were going in all along the line; Bostons and Hurricanes were bombing and machine-gunning the Dieppe defences, while others attacked the Rommel, Goering and Hitler batteries. Even then the Germans did not seem to anticipate a greater danger, and there was no general alert. The sight of the Bostons going in against the Goebbels battery had given heart to Major Young's small party as they lay on the top of the cliffs at Belleville.

At ten minutes past five o'clock curtains of smoke were laid over the Bismarck headland, and maintained effectively until six o'clock. At the same time bombing attacks went in against the hotels and boarding houses lining the Boulevard de Verdun. The enemy was at last aroused. Flight Lieutenant J. E. Scott, leading his formation of Blenheims into the attack against the East headland, had his jaw shattered by A/A fire, but he continued to lead his formation, pressing the attack home, though unable to speak through his intercommunication system.

But even at six o'clock there was no opposition in the air. Enemy air reconnaissance was below normal, and it was not until six o'clock that the German Air Force had its first alert. German pilots had been out on late passes. They had slept in billets away from their aerodromes. Over all that section of the French coast at this period of highest alertness men had undressed and gone to their beds.

Throughout all the period of the landings the R.A.F. were able to give maximum support to the men on the beaches in face of heavy A/A fire, but without hindrance in the sky. Even an hour later, at seven o'clock, there were not more than thirty German fighters, mostly F.W. 190's, in the air to do battle.

At that time Air Marshal Leigh-Mallory was beginning to fear that his challenge would not be taken. It was the greatest challenge of the war, and the bait of more than two hundred small ships, necessarily in close formation off Dieppe, must have been hard to refuse. It was, in fact, a gesture of extraordinary defiance, even of impudence, but following their defeat in the Battle of Britain the German Air Force were wary, even with all the advantages in their favour of fighting in their own air.

By seven o'clock repeated and urgent requests to the R.A.F. to lay more smoke over the headlands, and to attack the batteries, made it clear that all was not going well with our forces on the ground. These early demands for more smoke were the only ones that could not be met, for all smoke-carrying aircraft were already away, and it would be at least forty minutes before any more could be bombed up. Smoke must be planned in advance.

Meanwhile air attacks against the batteries and the headlands were redoubled, with Spitfires, Hurricanes and Bostons going in again and again with low-level attacks in the face of very heavy concentrations of A/A fire. Without support from the ground these attacks were not enough. The batteries Rommel, Goering and Hitler were not silenced, yet without the continuous harassing from the air it is probable that the large array of vessels off Dieppe would have suffered gravely.

Thus for five hours, comparatively unhindered in the air, sixty-seven squadrons of the R.A.F. flew sortie after sortie from their English fields, almost without mishap. Up to that time only one planned attack had failed to go in, when four out of six Hurricanes detailed to attack the German Divisional Headquarters at Arques la Bataille crashed on the ground. The remaining two aircraft failed to locate the target, which was hidden at that time under smoke.

It was not until ten o'clock that the German Air Force began to rise to the challenge in strength. It is, I suppose, conceivable that they had deliberately avoided the challenge in the early stages, leaving the task to the ground defences, and preferring to wait until the R.A.F. had begun to weary. Perhaps also they thought that this very large force might be the harbinger of invasion. It is certain that whatever the reasons for the very slow start, by ten o'clock the whole resources of the German Air Force in the West had been summoned to overwhelm the attackers. At least one hundred German fighters were in the air over the beaches and the sea, harassing our fighters and light bombers as they pressed home their attacks, while all the reserves of the German Fighter Air Force between Flushing and Beaumont le Roger had been alerted to instant action. At the same time all bomber forces based on Holland, Belgium and France were being committed to smash the landing craft and disrupt the whole fleet.

To meet this threat one wing of Typhoons of 12 Group made a diversionary feint over Ostend to draw off the bombers, and these were reinforced at first by three, then six, and finally by nine squadrons of Spitfires to intercept the large bomber forces moving South from Holland and Beauvais.

It was at this time, while the R.A.F. pilots, many of whom had already flown two, and even three, sorties out from England, met the first onslaught of this great enemy force, that they were called upon for their greatest efforts in support of the troops, and for the protection of the shipping. In the half hour from ten past ten o'clock to twenty minutes to eleven our fighters attacked machine-gun positions on the East and West headlands, while twenty-four Bostons and twenty-two Hurricane fighter-bombers did their uttermost to make an impression on these, as it seemed, almost impregnable natural fortresses.

The strain of the long ordeal was beginning to tell on the R.A.F. pilots, but they could not let up. The fighters against them were fresh, and with the advantage of being able to remain longer in the air, but in the one and a half hours of the withdrawal from eleven o'clock to half past twelve o'clock they had to lay smoke-screens, defend the whole convoy, protect the landing craft from intense enemy bomber efforts, and at the same time to fight the greatest single air battle of the war.

The deeds and tenacity of these young men are revealed in a few of the records of that day, exemplified by the case of Flying Officer Cholewke. Cholewke flew in No. 317 Polish Squadron. He was on his third sortie, already a weary man, when he went to the rescue of a Spitfire attacked by two F.W. 190's over the beaches. Wounded in the right arm in the first seconds, Cholewke succeeded in drawing off the enemy fighters, and fought a terrific duel, gaining precious seconds for the Spitfire pilot to recover height and initiative. Again Cholewke was wounded, this time in the right leg, but it was the dying shot of the beaten enemy.

It looked then to those who observed this battle in the air that Cholewke was lost as his Hurricane stalled, and seemed to hang for a moment like a wounded bird. Cholewke had lost consciousness. He regained his senses in time to right his aircraft, but lost consciousness a second time as he struggled home. Eventually he landed his aircraft at Lympne barely conscious, holding the control column between his knees and controlling the undercarriage mechanism with his left foot.

Over Dieppe and Pourville in that period of withdrawal, while Blenheims, Bostons and Hurricanes went in again and again against the headlands, the Spitfire pilots smashed the enemy bomber formations, and fought their dog fights in and out of the thickening cloud. Often then they were outnumbered two to one by pilots coming fresh to the battle. In that hour one Belgian fighter pilot was flying his fourth sortie. Many squadrons were flying their third. And in that period not one single enemy bomber succeeded in attacking either the landing craft or the great array of ships offshore.

But for the chance bomb that sank H.M.S. *Berkeley*, and the few enemy fighters able to disengage for long enough to press home their rare machine-gunning attacks, the whole naval force was unmolested.

From ten o'clock onwards the enemy tried every possible device to break through. At eleven o'clock bombers were spotted flying at ten to twelve thousand feet, protected by F.W. 190's at fifteen thousand feet. At once two squadrons of Spitfires were ordered to climb to twenty-three thousand feet to break up the formations. The official record reads: 'Two squadrons of Spitfires sent to deal with them at twenty-three thousand feet, and dealt with them.'

But by noon the losses on both sides had been heavy. The Air-Sea Rescue launches, answering calls for aid, were swooping in at speed under the coastal guns to pick pilots out of the water. The Mustangs, flying unarmed on Tactical Reconnaissance and penetrating deep into enemy territory in the search for troop movements, had suffered most heavily in proportion to their numbers. Ten of these aircraft had been lost. Relying on speed for their safety, and normally returning to England after their sorties, they had rendered themselves especially vulnerable by flying low over H.M.S. *Calpe* in their determination to get their information through.

Over the sea the naval gunners had brought down a mixed bag of twenty-nine bombers and fighters, including five of our own through faulty recognition. Eight bombers and smoke layers had been lost, and at least seventy Spitfires were down.

Meanwhile the enemy had lost at least forty bombers, and probably eighty. Nearly one hundred and fifty of their aircraft were certainly damaged. It might be months, or even years, before the final score was known, but that the R.A.F. were winning there was no doubt.

Despite their weariness our pilots had gained the upper hand soon after one o'clock. They had met every request from the Military and Naval Force Commanders to the limits of possibility, and had even anticipated most of them. The smooth flow of information that had come from Air Commodore Cole and his Observers throughout the day had kept No. 11 Group fully informed, and had enabled all demands to be met promptly. From first to last communications from aircraft to ship and from ship to Fighter Command Headquarters had been maintained. Only in the reverse direction had communications proved difficult, and at times non-existent.

And at last, free of their major commitments of support and protection, the R.A.F. pilots found the strength to dominate the sky over the Channel through all the hours of daylight.

At half past ten o'clock that morning twenty-four Flying Fortresses of the U.S. Army Air Force, escorted by four squadrons of Spitfires, had made a valuable contribution to the battle at a crucial time, by attacking the airfield at Abbeville. As a result the aerodrome had been unusable for two hours, and when it came again into operation new voices were speaking from the control towers. It is probable that all the original controllers were killed, and that the control of the aerodrome was virtually out of action all day.

Soon after one o'clock it had become apparent that the entire German Air Force in the West, now i. lly committed to the battle, was strained to the limits. If it had been possible to maintain the fight over the beaches it is almost certain that the Germans would have suffered their greatest defeat of the war in the air, and would have been forced to call upon their reserves from the East. But inevitably, as Operation Vanquish reached its conclusion and the whole fleet turned for home, the major air battle ended also. The need for the R.A.F. to maintain air cover over the ships, many of which were virtually defenceless, had grown rather than diminished, and the Germans would not be lured out to sea with their fighter strength.

The weather had deteriorated steadily throughout the day, and by a quarter to four o'clock, when this tremendous feat of organization in the air had been sustained in perfect rhythm for fully twelve hours, the enemy were able to profit by the cloud cover to harass the ships.

To meet the threat of the enemy bombers operating singly, the R.A.F. sent out eighty-six additional patrols, and the enemy lost heavily in this last phase without achieving any successes.

Fourteen bombers and sixteen fighters were brought down in mid Channel, and close to the English coast. The probables and the damaged more than doubled that number.

By nightfall, when the battle finally ended, and the little ships were emerging from the minefields to meet their escorts and come safely into harbour, the R.A.F. had flown 2,617 sorties, and lost a total of one hundred and six aircraft, eighty-eight of them Spitfires. The enemy finally admitted to the loss of one hundred and seventy aircraft, and it was estimated that between one quarter and one half of the German Air Force in the West had been put *hors de combat*. All this between dawn and dusk of that tragic day of the 19th August. It was the greatest clash of the Air Forces in a single day of the whole war. It hammered home the early promise of Dunkirk, when a handful of fighter squadrons had staved off a great weight of attack from an enemy imagining himself invincible. It confirmed the great victory of the Battle of Britain, and destroyed the last illusions of the German Air Force.

The experience of the Dieppe Raid was the final touch. The R.A.F. had given, as they had promised, complete air cover to by far the largest and most ambitious operation of its kind to be conceived up to that time. They were masters, and not only in their own sky. Their morale had become sublime.

Meanwhile on the sea the crews of the Air-Sea Rescue launches had shown a complete contempt for danger. In answering forty-seven calls for aid, mostly close in to the French coast, they had rescued thirteen pilots uninjured, and one wounded observer. They had also picked two more pilots out of the sea, one of whom was dead, and the other dying of wounds. The effort had cost them dear. Three high-speed launches were lost, and they had suffered a total of thirty-seven casualties, officers and men, including ten officers and five other ranks killed, eight wounded and fourteen missing.

In those days men paid willingly with their lives for the lives of pilots, often giving two and even three lives for one. In the harsh accounting of war it was not too much

The R.A.F. lost one hundred and thirteen pilots killed and missing, and forty wounded. The sacrifice was great, but in the air battle the reward was victory.[1]

[1] Appendix 6. Air Force Order of Battle—sectors.

CHAPTER TWENTY

RETURN TICKET

THE Dieppe Raid has been referred to in official quarters as the largest 'Return Ticket' operation of its kind to be conceived and carried out up to that time. The phrase, I feel, is at least an unhappy one, and with a note of rather bitter irony. It was a one-way journey for so many, and of those who did return nearly eight hundred were wounded, not a few to the point of death.

Throughout the whole day and night of the Raid the medical treatment had been confined of necessity to the first principles of saving life, that is to anti-shock treatment, the arrest of haemorrhage, warmth and food. Wounds, of course, were well and skilfully dressed, but there had been a shortage of large surgical dressings, so that the medical officers and orderlies, working under conditions of danger, discomfort and difficulty, had need to improvise. That they did so with resource and tireless devotion goes without saying, yet it is worth emphasising. It is always so, yet it seems a miracle that it is always so to those who have observed the behaviour of medical personnel under fire.

Many gravely wounded men on that day off Dieppe and on the beaches owed their lives not simply to medical skill and care, but to that calm brand of courage and disregard of danger and of self that is characteristic of the medical services in war. No men walk or work more calmly under shot and shell, and it was so throughout all that day on the beaches of Dieppe, on the seas off Dieppe, and on the long journey home. It had been a seemingly endless day and night of physical strain.

The first of the wounded had begun to come aboard H.M.S. *Calpe* and H.M.S. *Fernie* soon after half past four o'clock in the morning, although these were not in any real sense hospital ships. Indeed, the equipment necessary to transform Hunt class destroyers to Headquarters ships had still further limited the small space normally available for wounded.

Nevertheless the great weight of dealing with the bulk of the wounded fell on the destroyers, primarily *Calpe* and *Fernie*, and on the gun boat *Locust*. With a quarter of her own crew suffering wounds, *Calpe* took on board a total of two hundred and seventy-eight others. Long before nine o'clock they overflowed the wardroom and the after mess-deck, and there was no deck cover available for the majority. Through most of the day the wounded lay out on the decks with little or no protection from near misses and flying splinters. Inevitably many suffered graver wounds, and virtually both the wounded and those who attended them were under fire all day.

Owing to the nature of the disaster the numbers of the wounded did not exceed expectations, and were at no time unmanageable. But they were not unmanageable solely because the medical officers and orderlies declined to accept such a possibility, and drove themselves cheerfully beyond the bounds of normal endurance.

From dawn to well after noon *Calpe* and *Fernie* were besieged by small vessels, and answered all the heavy demands made upon them, while performing their own warlike roles with great skill. All this was due to the failure to seize and to hold the beaches and to establish bridgeheads. Four tank landing craft and two large flak landing craft had been prepared and equipped for wounded. Each of the four tank landing craft carried two medical officers and attendant orderlies, and each of the flak landing craft one medical officer and orderlies.[1] The intention was to ground the flak landing craft on the beaches one hour before the withdrawal was due to begin, and then to load them up to capacity. Each craft could take one hundred stretcher cases and sixty walking wounded. As soon as they were loaded up the craft would return to the Hards at Stokes Bay, where arrangements had been made to receive them, and convey the cot cases at once to hospital.

In the event none of this happened. From time to time the tank landing craft, which lay well out to sea awaiting the call to go in, answered urgent requests from destroyers and gun boats for medical officers, orderlies and supplies, and that was the total of their participation.

At ten minutes to nine o'clock, as soon as it had become clear to the Naval and Military Force Commanders that the beaches were not securely held, the four hospital tank landing craft were ordered to return to port.

Of the two large flak landing craft one did good service as a

[1] Appendix 7.

medical ship, and the other was sunk. This was the large Flak Landing Craft 2, which closed the main beaches in support of the landings at point-blank range. Lt. Graham fought his ship until he was killed, and it was then that Surgeon-Lt. L. P. Martin, M.R.C.S., finding himself the senior surviving officer, had fought the vessel until one by one her guns were silenced, and the vessel sank under him. Martin, wounded himself, took to the water with his sick berth ratings and fourteen wounded men, and succeeded in inspiring them all to keep afloat until they were finally rescued and taken on board *Calpe*.

Many of the medical personnel suffered wounds, and all who were able, including Surgeon-Lt. Martin, continued to tend the wounded all through the day and the following night. Among those who distinguished themselves for their 'indefatigable labours' was Corporal Comfort, who did not, states the official record, 'belie his name on that day'. Others earning special mention for their extreme devotion were Captain D. W. Clare and the Naval Chaplain, the Rev. W. V. Foote, B.A., on board *Calpe*.

When the bulk of the ships finally turned for home following the withdrawal there were few without some quota of wounded men. Fortunately the passage proved uneventful but for the continuous and unsuccessful attempts of the enemy to press home his attacks from the air.

It was after midnight when the destroyers, with *Calpe* and the *Locust* bringing up the rear, reached Portsmouth. By that time the whole convoy of more than two hundred little ships had been safely escorted into Newhaven, where many craft had to lie off-shore for hours with wounded on board, while waiting for harbour space.

In fact the arrangements for the reception of the wounded had broken down. Cot cases had to be hoisted out of the small craft by crane at Newhaven, and laboriously brought on shore. To make matters worse the hospital train, which had been made available, was routed for Birmingham, and cases in need of urgent surgical attention suffered many painful hours of waiting and travel.

The official comment drily states the obvious: 'Hospitals in the immediate vicinity should be used in preference to ones further away, even if not of the same service or unit.' (Birmingham is 160 miles from Newhaven.)

But at Portsmouth the reception was, if anything, worse.

In view of the conditions prevailing at Newhaven the Naval Force Commander decided to proceed to Portsmouth with the destroyer force at full speed, and signalled the Naval Commander-in-Chief Portsmouth accordingly. Further, the Naval Force Commander was uncertain of his time of arrival.

Faced with this emergency the Naval Commander-in-Chief Portsmouth took advantage of his powers as Regional Commissioner and assembled all the ambulance services in the County within the dockyard. At the same time wards were cleared at the Royal Naval Hospital at Haslar, and all available doctors were standing by.

Despite these efforts the result tried the nerves and resources of those who had already suffered greatly. When *Calpe* and *Locust* came alongside soon after midnight they had five hundred and fifty wounded men crowding their decks.

'Many kindly and enthusiastic people,' says the Report, 'were there to receive them.'

It was urged by these willing helpers that the wounded must be disembarked first, and this was agreed to. The Naval Force Commander went ashore immediately with his Staff from *Calpe*, while the crews of the destroyers remained on board. Stretchers had to be manhandled at acute angles up companionways while able-bodied men, themselves desperately tired, blocked the decks. Those who were landed first were at once loaded into ambulances and rushed to the Royal Naval Hospital at Haslar, irrespective of the type and urgency of their wounds. Because the least severely wounded were in the first flights, by the time the more gravely wounded were got ashore all the available hospital beds had been filled.

It was long after daylight when the last wounded man was on dry land.

Commenting briefly on the decision to remove the wounded from the destroyers at Portsmouth before disembarking the crews and able-bodied men, the official record states:

> This is obvious nonsense for, with upwards of two hundred men on the deck of a destroyer, the collection and disembarkation of walking wounded and stretcher cases is well-nigh impossible.

In common with many of the lessons learned from the Dieppe Raid it seems rather surprising that this lesson had not been learned some years earlier.

Of the two hundred and fifty-two ships that had sailed out of their four South Coast ports so hopefully in the dusk of the 18th August only thirty-four were lost, and of these all were landing craft of various kinds, except for the Hunt class destroyer, H.M.S. *Berkeley*. The losses in blood had far outweighed the losses in material.[1]

It all took some time to sort out. In the final ordeal of the withdrawal troops and craft had become seriously tangled, and it was six days before the casualties were known. For some days afterwards soldiers and sailors were found asleep on ships, or were picked up wandering, dazed and bewildered about the ports where they had landed, and with little or no idea of who they were or where they were.

In the final count the Canadian casualties alone reached a total of 215 Officers and 3,164 Other Ranks, out of a Canadian force engaged of under five thousand men. Little remained of the 4th Canadian Infantry Brigade, and not much more of the 6th. Les Fusiliers Mont-Royal, largely due to Sergeant Dubuc, was the only one of the seven major Canadian units engaged to bring its Commanding Officer back to England. The losses in senior officers alone was a great blow to the Canadian 2nd Division and to the 1st Canadian Corps.

Although these were the bulk of the casualties the crews of the landing craft had lost even more heavily in proportion. None had been more vulnerable at the landings and at the withdrawal.

The last entry in the German War Diary at the Headquarters of the Commander-in-Chief in the West, Field Marshal von Runstedt, reads:

19 Aug. 42.

1740 hours: No armed Englishman remains on the Continent.

So ended one of the most controversial exploits in the story of warfare. It had been decided to 'play it down'. Instead the Dieppe Raid touched off perhaps the greatest propaganda battle of the war.

[1] See Appendices 4 and 5.

PART THREE

AFTERMATH

CHAPTER TWENTY-ONE

THE PROPAGANDA BATTLE

I

THE first shots in the propaganda battle of the Dieppe Raid were fired by the B.B.C. in their early morning broadcast to the people of Dieppe shortly after the first landings. This broadcast urged the people to remain calm; to take no part in the affair and to understand that it was simply a Raid, and not an attempt at invasion.

The accent on the nature of the operation as a Raid was of vital importance, for it was realized that the Germans would almost certainly attempt to turn the landings, whether they were successful or not, into a frustrated attempt at invasion. To get in first was therefore of great importance, and with this early broadcast of the 19th August the British seized the propaganda initiative.

No 1 Communiqué was issued at six o'clock in the morning, 19th August, from Combined Operations Headquarters.

'RAID OVER FRANCE

'A raid was launched in the early hours of to-day on the Dieppe area of enemy Occupied France.

The Operation is still in progress, and a further communiqué will be issued when fuller reports are available.

Meanwhile the French people are being advised by wireless broadcasts that this raid is not an invasion.'

The second communiqué from Combined Operations Headquarters was issued at two minutes to one o'clock, 19th August, as follows:

'The troops taking part in the raid on the Dieppe area have landed at all the points selected. Heavy opposition was encountered in some places, and on the left flank one landing

169

party was initially repulsed but reformed and later carried the beach by assault.

The troops on the right flank, having achieved their objective, which included the complete destruction of a six-gun battery and ammunition dump, have now been re-embarked. In the centre tanks were landed and heavy fighting is proceeding.

The Military Force consists mainly of Canadian troops. Also taking part are British Special Service troops, a detachment from a U.S. Ranger Battalion, and a small contingent of Fighting French.

This force was carried and escorted by units of the Royal Navy. Air support and protection on a large scale is being provided by bomber and fighter aircraft of the Royal Air Force in the face of considerable enemy opposition.

A further communiqué will be issued later.'

Unfortunately this communiqué was held up for some hours by censorship, and the enemy was enabled to get in first with the mention of tanks.

The first enemy broadcast at noon addressed to German listeners in Norway was otherwise innocuous. There was no hint of the invasion line to be followed by the enemy, and this was probably a mistake:

'The British in the early hours of this morning made a landing on the French channel coast supported by considerable numbers of air and naval forces. The British, who have landed infantry and tanks, met hard and successful resistance of German troops.'

By the evening of the 19th August the battle had begun to take shape, and the people of Dieppe were amused to receive the congratulations of Marshal Pétain for their behaviour. Two hours later Hitler's praise and personal thanks were broadcast from the Headquarters of the German High Command, and early on the morning of the 20th August the British added their thanks and praise.

This was, perhaps, the only point on which Vichy, Germany and Britain were agreed, and it was developed as a strong side-line by Hitler, bringing considerable benefits to the people of Dieppe as time went on. It is not, perhaps, altogether unpleasant to be wooed even by the Devil.

The propaganda offensive which now began to emerge from German broadcasters was one of the most ambitious and prolonged campaigns devised by the enemy. By nightfall on the 19th August Britain had lost the propaganda initiative, and it was not regained.

2

The British Public Relations Plan had envisaged propaganda elements which the enemy might use against us:[1]

(i) Assumption by anyone that this raid was an invasion attempt.

(ii) Efforts by the enemy to misinterpret any statement on action by us and represent the raid as an invasion attempt which was repulsed.

(iii) Vagueness about the objectives of the raid. Such vagueness might be used by the enemy to belittle the results of the raid.

It had also considered some new propaganda factors which had not previously arisen in Combined Operations Raids.

(i) The large number of troops involved.

(ii) Canadian and American troops were being used for the first time in a raid.

(iii) The use of tanks with the result that the enemy might use captured and disabled tanks as evidence of a so-called 'Repulsed Second Front'.

(iv) The fact that the news of the raid would be issued while our troops were still in action and still in touch with the local population during daylight hours.

There were also some important factors to be considered in

[1] Comd. C.B. 04244, paras. 1238, 1239, 1240.

maintaining the offensive in propaganda at all times. Primarily it was essential to emphasize:

(i) That this was a *raid*, not an invasion attempt.
(ii) That although on a larger scale than before, it had certain limited objectives.
(iii) That a large number of Canadian troops and some American troops were taking part.
(iv) That our objectives should be announced as and when achieved.
(v) That the fact that the tanks were used should be announced to prevent enemy from making capital out of his own disclosure of their use.

It was further intended that the operation should be 'played down' as much as possible in order to keep it in its proper perspective in relation to the fighting in other theatres of war. No Press interviews were therefore to be permitted with the fighting personnel of any of the Services taking part in the raid, except specially selected cases.

Nine war correspondents had been carried on the raid, four of them American, three Canadian and two British. It was hoped that they would be able to counteract mis-statements from enemy eye-witness accounts. In fact they saw very little. Two were wounded, and only three landed, one with the Royal Regiment, one with the South Saskatchewan Regiment, and one with No. 4 Commando.

Several further points of great importance had been thought of in advance, and the most important of these was the participation of American troops. It was fully appreciated at Combined Operations Headquarters that 'the historic implication of the first U.S. troops landing on French soil since 1917' would carry a powerful Press impact.

Steps were taken to ensure that this should not happen. It was made clear to the American people that United States officers participated in planning the raid, and all United States releases of news were made by the United States Army Headquarters in London.

Considerable discussion then took place as to the disclosure of the actual number of American troops, but since the number was so small it was decided not to mention numbers. This was a mistake, as it turned out.

There was great anxiety on this point of the use of Americans, and it is apparent in a note Combined Operations Headquarters received from the Personal Secretary to the Foreign Secretary urging that the part played by U.S. troops in the operation should not be over-stressed, since over-emphasis of their participation might harm Anglo-American relations.

These fears were swiftly realized. Despite the issue of news through United States Army Headquarters, and the emphasis on the small numbers of American troops, United States newspapers headlined the operation as an American show, and played it up to the delight of the enemy and the chagrin of the Allies. At the same time, the British Press, hungry for something positive to pin their stories upon, jumped at the success of No. 4 Commando and gave the impression that it was a Commando show. Even the vital news of the great battles on the Russian front was pushed off the front pages and relegated to snippets of news on the inside.

In the whole Allied Press the Dieppe Raid was divided between the Americans of whom there were fifty, most of whom did not land, and No. 4 Commando with their successful attack on the right flank. The Canadians were virtually ignored.

Once the newspapers on both sides of the Atlantic were in full cry with these misleading trends and statements it was difficult—indeed it proved impossible—to stop them. The appetites of editors and public had been whetted by the preliminaries, and big news there had to be.

It would not be difficult to be wise after the event, and to lash about with scorn at the Public Relations failure, but the real blame lies at the door of the operation itself. It failed to provide any real hard news in time, and no one, it seemed, had considered the possibility of failure. There was a vacuum, and it was filled.

The main fault of Public Relations[1] seems always to be a tendency to excessive caution which usually results in getting the worst of both worlds. Also, it tends to regard the Press as an enemy, or at least with suspicion. This may be justified, but it is unwise. At any rate from the British point of view the official communiqués and guidance were dull, late, and with the Commandos giving the only ring of success.

[1] Press relations is, perhaps, more apt.

It is not difficult, I think, to understand how the British newspapers came to emphasize the Commandos out of all proportion to the size of the Raid, but it is hard to understand how the American newspapers came to headline the story as virtually an American operation, and to give an impression that has probably stuck in many American minds ever since. The small number of American troops taking part was constantly and carefully—doubtless too carefully—indicated in all cables referring to the Raid. It was, of course, a mistake not to have given the actual numbers in the first place, but the Americans were very touchy at the time, and any reference to the actual figure might have been misconstrued.

The official record of this phase of the propaganda story makes it clear that a Press Guidance memo should have been issued by the United States Army Headquarters to the American Press. At any rate, by the 21st August the headlines were blazing, and nothing could stop them, while at home every effort was made by Public Relations to keep the part played by the 'Commandos' in proper perspective, but these efforts also failed.

These things not only gave the public a completely false impression of the Dieppe Raid, but also created resentments in the Army and with the sorely hurt Canadians.

As late as the 30th August the Prime Minister sent the following memorandum to the Secretary of State for War:

'It is natural that there should be some resentment in the Army at the undue emphasis laid upon the work of the Commandos by the Press. Your Press Officers should point out to the newspapers the ill effects which are caused by, for instance, referring to the raid on Dieppe in which numerous battalions of Canadian troops took part as a "Commando Raid". This is neither fair to the troops nor to the Commandos.'

But these propaganda troubles, great as they were, were on the home front. They did not seriously affect the trend of political warfare rapidly developed by the enemy, and which had begun to rage at full blast within forty-eight hours of the Raid.

On the 20th August the Prime Minister himself had come to the rescue of Public Relations by supplying the phrase 'a reconnaissance in force' aptly to describe the scope of the Raid. The

Germans were quick to retaliate with the slogan, 'Too large to be a symbol, too small to be a success.'

From his Headquarters in the West Field Marshal von Runstedt issued the following statement, referring to:

'THE GREAT ENEMY LANDING

'The operation at Dieppe cannot be considered a local raid. For this the expenditure in men and materials is too great. One does not sacrifice twenty to thirty of the most modern tanks for a raid.

Much rather is it to be assumed that, by employing such considerable forces, the enemy thought to effect a rapid seizure of the Dieppe bridgehead, after elimination of the artillery defences, in order then to utilize the good port facilities for bringing up and landing in succession the floating and operational reserves.

He will not do it like this a second time.'

The last words were true enough, and it seems that von Runstedt, although he could have been in no possible doubt that it was in fact a raid,[1] may have genuinely over-estimated the forces involved. His estimate was that there were between three and four hundred landing craft, protected by thirteen to fifteen cruisers and destroyers.

By the night of 19th August, long before all the ships were home, and while we were groping for something to say, and hesitating to say it, the Germans were developing three main lines of propaganda attack:

(i) Complete failure of the operation.
(ii) A desperate attempt to open a Second Front.
(iii) The last-minute outcome of political necessity and pressure.

And of these the last was the most deadly.

Unfortunately, Mr. Churchill had paid a visit to Moscow only twelve days before the Raid, and the news had been released only one day before. The juxtaposition of these events, which had no

[1] See below. Capture of 'Jubilee' Plan.

bearing whatever upon each other, was extremely unfortunate. It was a most potent gift to the enemy, and he was already almost overburdened with ammunition.

3

The whole tone of the first communiqué issued from Combined Operations Headquarters, cautious as it was, could not fail to excite editors. The fact of the emphasis on the operation as a Raid, coupled with the warning to the French people that it was not an invasion, was almost certain to create a feeling that this might be the Second Front for which almost everyone was waiting anxiously. The denial might not even ring true to British ears, and one does not need to be an editor to smell a big story in the preliminaries.

There was, I think, only one course to follow, and that was to provide a steady flow of news to editors, and to take them as much as possible into the confidence of Combined Operations, and to trust to their judgment. Few people know better how to make the best of a bad job. Security is often a two-edged sword, and the long delay in the release of the second communiqué left a dangerous vacuum.

By the evening of the 19th August the Germans had weighed up the situation, and a remarkable plum had fallen into their laps. With the capture of Brigadier Southam on White Beach 121 pages of the detailed Military Plan of "Jubilee" had fallen into their hands. The complete plan runs to 199 pages, but the Germans had enough to understand fully the nature of the operation, and one paragraph in particular in regard to prisoners was to lead to repercussions of the gravest kind. But this did not affect the propaganda pattern of the first few days.

Before the second British communiqué had been released to the Press, and with the newspapers and public waiting hungrily for news through all that day, a statement was broadcast from the Führer's Headquarters at half past eight o'clock on the 19th.

This broadcast was factual and reasonably reserved until the last paragraph, which seemed clearly the work of Hitler himself. The raid was referred to as 'only serving political purposes' and as an 'annihilating defeat'. The broadcast wound up as follows:

'The German watch in the West has given suitable rebuff to the amateur undertaking. Moreover it is awaiting any further attempts by the enemy with the calm and strength of an armed force which in hundreds of battles has added victory to its pennants.'

Two hours later Edward Dietze broadcast in English from Breslau, and stressed the 'disastrous failure' of 'this desperate expedient', which had been 'decided upon for purely political reasons by an unscrupulous and vainglorious amateur, driven to despair by the urgent demands of the Kremlin.'

There had been, said the Germans, a 'twelve-day ultimatum' from Stalin to Churchill to start a Second Front, and that was the real explanation of Mr. Churchill's visit to Moscow.

The political warfare angle was now quite clear, and it rapidly gained in importance over the military presentation.

In England the sequence of events moved soberly with the issue of Press Guidance to Editors—Not for Publication, throughout the day of the 19th. The first of these guidance notes was issued at half past one o'clock on the 19th from Controller: Press and Censorship:

'Following the news of the Combined Operations Raid on Dieppe certain factors which for obvious reasons could not be previously disclosed are given for your guidance. The present raid, in which a more numerous personnel is taking part than on previous raids and in which tanks are being used for the first time marks an important step forward in the planned programme of our agreed offensive policy. It is important in commenting on the raid to bear this fact in mind.'

The guidance continued:

'. . . it is difficult to estimate the probable losses we shall incur, but in any case our losses must be seen not only in their relation to German losses in men, material and aircraft, but also in the light of the invaluable experience gained in the employment of substantial forces and in the transport of heavy equipment.

While Canadian troops comprise the main body of the

landing force, they constitute approximately one third of the total personnel of all services participating.'

This was not very helpful, and at fifteen minutes past nine o'clock on the night of the 19th further guidance was issued:

'During the Combined Operations Raid on Dieppe an epic air battle developed comparable with those during the Battle of Britain. The enemy has constantly refused to give battle on this scale since those days. The result is particularly satisfactory to us when one realizes that we were fighting tied to the protection of our own forces seventy miles across the sea.'

The story of the air battle was then stressed and developed, and good though it was it did not give editors the kind of shot and shell they so urgently needed.

The Press Guidance concluded:

'It is hoped that in comments on the operation against Dieppe the results of this air battle will not be allowed to overshadow those achieved by the land and sea fighting.'

And at last, in time for the morning papers of the 20th August, No. 2 Communiqué was released; followed by No. 3:

'Despite the clear statement issued in our first communiqué this morning and broadcast to the French at 6.15 a.m. about the Raid on Dieppe, German propaganda, unable to make other capital out of the turn the operation has taken, is claiming that the raid was an invasion attempt which they have frustrated.

In point of fact the re-embarkation of the main forces was begun six minutes after the time scheduled, and it has been completed in nine hours after the initial landing, as planned.

Some tanks have been lost during the action ashore and reports show that fighting has been very fierce and that casualties are likely to have been heavy on both sides. Full reports will not be available until our forces are back in England.'

There followed a brief statement on the destruction of the six-gun battery behind Quiberville, together with other damage done, and an emphasis of enemy casualties, and finally the air battle.

The first three communiqués were now in the hands of editors, and the exact emphasis of 'six minutes' was a good point. A long vacuum followed. This was, of course, filled by the Germans, and inevitably people hungry for news listened, albeit critically, to the broadcasts of 'Lord Haw-Haw'. That the Dieppe Raid was in fact an invasion feint at the very least was firmly planted in the minds of most people.

Owing to the lack of information no briefing conference was held until fifteen minutes to eleven o'clock on the morning of the 20th. The war correspondents were restlessly anxious to write their stuff, and at noon these accounts were to be released. There was then a further delay while these were submitted to Censorship, and it was finally five minutes past six o'clock on the evening of the 20th before the first 'eye-witness' accounts were available. This, of course, was much too late for the evening papers. The Royal Air Force stories had also been held up for simultaneous release, but by that time 'Commando' headlines had dominated the newspapers, and a plea for further emphasis on Canadian predominance issued at six o'clock was virtually ignored. It was followed by a further piece of guidance at ten minutes past nine o'clock:

'It will be very much appreciated if in these stories of the Combined Operations Raid on Dieppe, the newspapers will bear in mind that by far the biggest proportion of the troops engaged were Canadian forces.

To emphasize Commandos in headlines and stories would be to give an unfair perspective of the operation.'

No. 4 Communiqué was issued at ten minutes to eleven o'clock on the night of the 20th.

'Reports now received from Force Commanders make it possible to give a full co-ordinated story of the Combined Operations Raid in the Dieppe area.

These reports show that as a combined operation the raid was a successful demonstration of co-ordination of all three services.'

The communiqué developed this theme justly, though in schoolboy language 'it was a fat lot of use'; and continued:

'The Raid had as its objectives: The testing by an offensive on a larger scale than previously of the defences of what is known to be a heavily defended sector of the coast, the destruction of German batteries, of a Radiolocation station which plays an important part in the German attacks on our Channel convoys, the destruction of German Military personnel and equipment, and the taking of prisoners for interrogation. The raid was a reconnaissance in force, having a vital part in our agreed offensive policy.'

There followed a description of the things achieved and some facts of the air battle. The communiqué ended:

'As a result of the heavy fighting which developed during the operation our casualties were high, but not unduly so in view of the operation.'

Meanwhile the Germans and their Allies had filled the unforgiving minutes of the 20th August. Paris Radio had referred to the British as 'fighting to the last Canadian', but this theme had not been followed up.

Broadcasting at fifteen minutes to seven o'clock on the German Home Service on the 20th August, Lt.-General Dittmar had struck a note not in tune with the developing trends of the political line, when he gave his opinion that at least ten months of planning lay behind the Dieppe Raid. He further commented that Germans should be grateful that the 'first landings succeeded, for if they had not then there would not have been possible such a complete British defeat'.

A slightly discordant note was also struck by Ansaldo, broadcasting from Italy on the evening of the 20th. Ansaldo said: 'In our considered opinion the British High Command did not even know what it hoped to achieve.'

In a broadcast at half past eight o'clock on the evening of the 20th Transocean fixed the 'Invasion' theme, and no commentator deviated thereafter.

Meanwhile a Vichy broadcast in English to the United States

was effective in spreading dangerous rumour. The broadcast stated that it is

'rumoured that the British, including American units, attempted two other landing operations in the neighbourhood of Brest and Bordeaux, both of which failed completely.

Barges, in which many thousand American and British troops were being ferried to Brest and Bordeaux, were sunk before reaching the coast. There are practically no survivors, it is reported. . . .'

By the 21st August the political theme outweighed the military, though the Germans were able to reinforce their military broadcasts with many carefully staged and dramatic eye-witness stories. These all emphasized the size of the force engaged and the extent of the catastrophe. Numerous photographs, of which our own cupboard was completely bare, helped their newspaper presentation.

The stuff poured out. On the morning of 21st August the German Home Service commented typically:

'From the whittling down of the abortive invasion to eulogizing it as a great success is only a small step for so gifted a liar as Churchill.'

Transocean broadcasting in English on the afternoon of the 22nd August said:

'Numerous reports on the immediate revival of Soviet propaganda in England bluntly asking Churchill what he intends to do for his Soviet ally are valued in Berlin as additional proof that Churchill will be unable to avoid giving additional invasion orders.'

It was also emphasized that probably the bulk of our Landing Force was in the background and that these were to have been thrown into the battle as soon as the first wave of landing troops had achieved the formation of a bridgehead around the Port of Dieppe.

'Lord Haw-Haw' described the Prime Minister as having to

divide his time between an attempt to execute instructions from Washington and in the vain endeavour to comply with the demands of Moscow.

Otto Krieg commented:

'Britain would have had to attempt some action of her own even without the strongest pressure from Stalin. Dependent upon American aid she had to demonstrate to Roosevelt her capacity for action.'

One of the small grains of comfort we had from all this rather telling stuff was that the Germans were shouting so loud that they had probably been rather more frightened than we had thought. Foreign reactions had not been entirely unfavourable, and as time went by some of these improved.

On the 19th August the Russians had withheld all news, except for stating that British aircraft operated over a wide area between Le Havre and Dieppe. The story finally made its impact upon the Russian people as a completed event, and not 'blow-by-blow'.

Robert Magidoff speaking from Moscow to the United States early on the 21st August said that he thought that the Russians were disappointed over Dieppe.

'They were hoping,' he said, 'this was the beginning of the Second Front. . . . Are the British waiting for the Germans to take the Caucasus to open the Second Front in Iran or India?

This is the question many Russians are asking. The Red Army is doing everything it can to prevent such a tragic Second Front.'

But Russian broadcasts firmly denied that it was an invasion attempt, and one comment was: 'It was simply a more precise testing of calculations connected with great and serious military operations to be undertaken in the near future.'

Ernest Fischer, speaking to Germany from Moscow, described the English and Americans as being 'able to land when they wish and where they wish. The Second Front is inescapable. This is the result of the Anglo-American reconnaissance raid.'

Tass put out a report in English on 21st August, and alleged to have come from Paris. This stated that the Germans had arrested two hundred French in the neighbourhood of Dieppe after the withdrawal. 'German circles say the arrests are due to the hostile attitude of certain French towards German troops.'

Tass later quoted Havas Agency as saying: 'The raid proves that the Channel can be crossed, troops landed and heavy equipment unloaded on one of the best defended parts of Northern France.'

Dieppe was the first use of armoured fighting vehicles in a landing and it began to be clear that this had made an impression, particularly in Sweden.

David Anderson broadcasting from Stockholm in the United States Home Service on the 20th August said:

'Here in the land of cold realism the Swedish Press is taking the raid on Dieppe as having the greatest importance. Bear in mind that the Swedish Press has been flooded by stories of the impossibility of an Allied landing on the French coast, and that as there was no evidence to dispute this claim, a portion of German propaganda has taken root in common Swedish conceptions.

But now what do we find?'

Anderson then continued with a long and vivid story of the Allied ability to cross the Channel in strength and land troops and fighting vehicles in the face of the strongest German defences.

The news from Turkey was not so good. Ankara was at first cautious, both Press and Wireless giving equal space and time to both sides. The balance then began to shift slightly in favour of Britain. Casualties on both sides were described as 'high', and the invasion story was denied. It was 'not an invasion but an experimental raid in which first-hand information was gained'. In this light, said Ankara, 'It was a signal success.'

These reactions were better than could have been expected, but the British case had rough treatment from Spain. Headlines proclaimed 'A New Dunkirk', 'Complete Failure' and a 'Sensational Collapse'. The German political warfare line was faithfully followed, and it was argued in the Spanish Press and on the

Radio that Dieppe came so close after the Moscow Conference
that the connection could not be mistaken.

Japan was the last of the important commentators. Broadcasting from Tokyo in Spanish for Latin-American listeners
Japanese spokesmen speculated about the American part in the
Raid, and considered that the inclusion of American troops was
more propagandist than military. The raid was cited as a proof of the
critical condition of the Russian army, and the commentator ended:

'Japanese military authorities say that when the English
make serious attempts at large scale operations of this sort
it will take a long time for the Germans to move troops from
East to West.'

Meanwhile the German hate campaign against Britain was
taking an unpleasant shape.

4

If there was any cause for satisfaction in this storm of enemy
propaganda touched off by the Dieppe Raid, it was that a certain
uneasiness could be detected. There was not much doubt that the
Germans were scared, and that von Runstedt's summing-up: 'He
will not do it like this again,' was cold comfort. That he would
'do it again' was undoubted; but when, where and how?

The reports coming from France were on the whole good. The
prisoners of Les Fusiliers Mont-Royal had sung 'La Marseillaise'
as they were marched through Rouen. It had gone to the hearts
of the people, and it was clear that new hopes had been kindled
by the Raid.

Probably because of these things, and the evident growing
unpopularity of the Germans, Hitler had developed his wooing of
the inhabitants of Dieppe in a quite remarkable manner, un-
warranted by anything they had done or had suffered on the day.
It was soon announced that all prisoners of war in German hands
from the Dieppe area would be released as a mark of the Führer's
appreciation. A policy of thanks and rewards was ordered for the
'perfect calm and discipline' of the people of Dieppe, and a
ten million franc relief fund was organized by General Stulpnagel.

These things were accepted with cynical pleasure by the Dieppois.

Towards the end of August a campaign of hate inspired by Goebbels himself had begun to dominate news and broadcasts, and it was apparent that the capture of the Military Plan of 'Jubilee' was developing grave and unlooked-for consequences. There is, in these orders, a brief passage referring to action in regard to prisoners taken on the Raid. In this passage it is advised that prisoners' hands should be tied to prevent them from destroying documents prior to interrogation. Other passages, referring to the retention of medals and badges of rank and the general treatment of any prisoners taken, make it clear that the highest standards of humanity were to be observed. Wounded, for example, were to be treated in exactly the same way as our own. There were no priorities.[1]

But the Germans were looking for trouble, and the paragraph about tying of hands, unfortunately included in the 121 pages of the captured plan, loosed a storm that was utterly bewildering. As a result the British prisoners taken on the raid were put in chains, and a campaign of brutalities was launched that was to culminate in the threatened shooting of our captured airmen.

There seems little doubt that the paragraph in the Jubilee Plan, innocuous as it would appear, was nevertheless strictly against the policy of the War Office, and should not have been put in. In fact the hands of prisoners taken had not been tied, even for short periods, and the War Office issued a denial that an intention to tie the hands of prisoners had ever been, or would be, British policy.

But the Germans had lashed themselves into a fury, and by so doing had shocked almost everyone but themselves. Their campaign of execration and hate did not ring true to anyone. The official record states: 'What seemed to be a minor occurrence has been seized by the enemy to justify the most brutal activities.'

There was little to be done, but to protest in the face of the growing orgy of hate as the words and deeds of the Germans took their terrible course. To retaliate in any way was unthinkable.

[1] Appendix 10.

5

In reviewing the results of the long propaganda battle Public Relations acknowledged many faults and learned some valuable lessons. The first of them was that Public Relations Planning must not be viewed by the Services as 'publicity preparations'. The whole attitude towards news and the Press must change, for the newspapers and broadcasting services are, in fact, 'services' themselves.

Even more necessary is it to provide a steady stream of news at all costs, and to do this alternative courses must be prepared beforehand. Vacuums are always dangerous, and are certain to be filled.

Finally Public Relations noted, rather obviously and pathetically, that,

'It is insufficient to prepare plans for success. If a long-term programme is to be carried on properly Public Relations Planning must include three possibilities: (a) Success, (b) partial success, (c) failure.'

The conclusions on political warfare were of greater interest. With the 'raid idea' we had a propaganda lead in the first hours, but

'The Plan for political warfare lapsed with the issue of the 3rd Communiqué. In the ensuing twenty-seven hours we lost the initiative that we had established and held for fifteen hours, and owing to the lack of any further material with which to cover angles from which we were being attacked, German propaganda built up a strong position in the field.

The enemy's political counter attack was reinforced by the addition of much detail, military and political. While public opinion in this country was being antagonized by the splashing of the Raid across whole sheets of newspapers whilst the Russian front was grudgingly accorded a bare, insignificant admission, the situation as regards political warfare to enemy and enemy occupied countries deteriorated as those countries

187

were deluged with Axis propaganda, Axis assertions and distortions.'¹

In sum, it was 'a bad moment'.
Official opinion was that

'the best thing from a political viewpoint would have been no Raid at that time; the next best, a sensational military success, and the very least requisite, the attainment of objectives so obviously important, and easy to explain to the Public that no doubt could remain as to the meaning of the operation.'

It may be of interest at this late hour that all my friends, knowing that I have been involved in this work, have asked the same question:
"Well, and was it an invasion attempt?"

¹ B.R. 1877, Combined Operations H.Q. October 1942.

CHAPTER TWENTY-TWO

SUCCESS OF A RECONNAISSANCE

THERE is no direct answer to the question, "Was the Dieppe Raid a success or a failure?" It was both. I think the operation must be considered from two clear standpoints, first as a Reconnaissance, and secondly as a Raid. As a Reconnaissance, 'Operation Jubilee' is a success; as a Raid it is a failure. A question must arise, I believe, as to whether the success is in any way due to the failure. It is a disturbing question in some ways.

The Prime Minister's phrase, 'A Reconnaissance in Force', so apt at the time, is perhaps also the truest description of 'Operation Jubilee'. In examining the results, the Plan and the Execution of the Raid, and particularly in any criticism of the Plan and the Execution, there is always, as it seems to me, an unknown factor: what are they really after?

The Reconnaissance is a success because one cannot doubt from the words of the Prime Minister, of Lt.-General H. D. G. Crerar, and others in a position to know, that it provided vital information which contributed in a high degree to the planning, and to the final success of the Normandy Landings. The Canadians have written in their war history:

'The casualties sustained in the Raid were part of the price paid for knowledge that enabled the great operation of 1944 to be carried out at a cost in blood smaller than even the most optimistic had ventured to hope for.'

One cannot, I think, quibble with that.

As a Naval operation it was a success. The Air Battle was a victory. The Military operation was a disaster.

However unfortunate the operation was from a political viewpoint one cannot doubt that a Raid on this scale was a military necessity at the time. I have quoted the Prime Minister (Sir Winston Churchill) in my prologue as saying that no responsible General would take the responsibility of planning for the main invasion until an operation on the scale of the Dieppe Raid had been undertaken. It was by far the most considerable operation of its kind up to that time, and the results enabled the 'responsible Generals' to go ahead with their planning for 'Overlord'.

That alone is a good enough reason for the Raid, and a considerable result.

The Canadians have stated that 'it is in the light of the success of Normandy that the Dieppe landings must be judged'. The Canadian sacrifice was immeasurably the greatest. So be it.

Even the immediate results were not inconsiderable. Great forces were set in motion by the Germans towards Dieppe and Pourville, and,

> 'Strategically,' the Prime Minister wrote, 'the Raid served to make the Germans more conscious of danger along the whole coast of Occupied France. This helped to hold troops and resources in the West, which did something to take the weight off Russia. Honour to the brave who fell. Their sacrifice was not in vain.'

The immediate effect on the morale of the Canadian Army was also great.

> 'There is no doubt whatever,' wrote Col. J. B. Stacey, 'that in the Army (Canadian) it produced a new sense of pride. There was less demand now for an immediate assault on the Germans in the West; the magnitude of such an enterprise was more clearly apparent than before, as was the need for the most detailed preparation, the more careful training, the most exacting discipline.'

The Raid also stilled much of the general clamour for a Second Front, which was at that time very widespread, and no doubt embarrassing. The fact that it needed two hundred and fifty-two ships and sixty-seven squadrons of aircraft to make a Raid of a few hours' duration with a landing force of six thousand men, sobered up casual and uninformed thinking. It made most people realize something of the enormous preparation and the staggering quantities of materials necessary to mount and sustain a real invasion.

Perhaps not the least of the important results was that it seems to have convinced the Germans that an invasion could be destroyed on the beaches. It also led them to believe that the Allies would concentrate on the capture of a major port, and therefore to concentrate their own defence efforts on the ports.

The Prime Minister (Sir Winston Churchill) wrote in his *Memoirs*:

'Looking back the casualties of this memorable action may seem out of proportion to the results. It would be wrong to judge the episode solely by such a standard. Dieppe occupies a place of its own in the story of war, and the grim casualty figures must not class it a failure. It was a costly but not unfruitful Reconnaissance in force. Tactically it was a mine of experience. It shed revealing light on many shortcomings in our outlook. It taught us to build in good time various types of craft and appliances for later use. We learnt again the value of powerful support by heavy naval guns in an opposed landing, and our bombardment technique, both marine and aerial, was thereafter improved.'

Finally the Prime Minister wrote:

'My general impression of "Jubilee" (Dieppe) is that the results fully justified the heavy cost. The large-scale air battle alone justified the Raid.'

Listed among the pre-eminent purposes of the Raid is the following:

'To test the German defences at a point on the coast where fighter cover could be provided, and to lure as much as possible of the German Air Force into the sky. These purposes were achieved. Between one quarter and one half of the German Air Force in the West was put *hors de combat*, and the defences were thoroughly tested.'

CHAPTER TWENTY-THREE

FAILURE OF A RAID

THE general conditions, the defences, and the enemy strength encountered at Dieppe and on the neighbouring beaches did not differ greatly from the expectation. Military Intelligence, aided by Air Reconnaissance, had built up a picture with care and thoroughness from a mass of material. It was sound and true in broad outline, and with much useful detail. Inevitably there were mistakes and omissions. The mistakes were, on the whole, unimportant. The omissions were no greater than a normal military imagination might have been expected to fill in. The worst of these omissions was the unknown strength of the East headland, Bismarck. The presence of the caves, both natural and artificial, was, of course, well known. That something was inside them, and something undoubtedly dangerous, was obvious.

The Intelligence report prior to the Raid states: 'It is impossible to deny or confirm machine-gun posts in the low cliffs East of harbour entrance.'

No one can doubt the potential power of this headland, but it seems to have been grossly underestimated.

I have embodied in my story all the information available on the defences and on the enemy weapons, and have drawn on the Intelligence summaries and the final reports of the Naval and Military Force Commanders for most of these facts. Many of these details were not known in advance, and one of the unhappy surprises was the enemy's extensive and devastating use of mortars. These weapons alone, it is estimated, accounted for approximately 32 per cent of the casualties suffered.

It was known in considerable detail that there were machine-gun casemates all along the coast, and that the numerous machine-gun posts were each of four guns and manned by approximately thirty men. Many machine-gun positions had also been detected on the roof tops of buildings. All this information, together with light A/A battery sites, was meticulously embodied on battle maps, and it was fully appreciated that Divisional artillery would support the fixed coastal batteries.

A good deal of the wire was revealed in photographs, but the dannert was of a heavier type than any we had previously encountered.

Enemy troops were also well assessed. The German 110 Division, with its Headquarters in the Château of Arques la Bataille, was thought to be holding the area. One battalion with ancillary troops usually held the town of Dieppe, and a total of 1,700 men might be expected there up to three hours. In the event, as I have mentioned in the body of my story, the area was held by 571 Regiment of the German 302 Division, with two battalions forward and one in reserve to a depth of seven miles.

302 Division had been reinforced throughout July and August, and was on normal routine alert for this period. The Casino defences had been strengthened as recently as the 10th August, but this had no special significance.

The post-war examination of the German records confirms that the enemy did not receive any warning of our intention to attack. We know also that the Guard of the Coastal Defence artillery was normal on the night, and that despite the Alert period, defence troops out on passes returned to Headquarters, undressed and went to sleep.

The reaction of the coastal batteries and the German Air Force was remarkably slow.

The first alarm was received at the Casino on the West front of Dieppe at five o'clock. The sounds of battle from Pourville were by that time unmistakable, and air attacks were going in.

The situation, therefore, at Dieppe and along the line of coast to be assaulted, was accurately appreciated. All the major factors were known to the planners in advance, and the state of readiness of the enemy was less than could have been expected. Even the unlucky clash of Group 5 with the armed trawlers had failed to give warning on shore. There were no surprises.

Through the night of the 18th–19th August the Royal Navy had performed a near miracle of seamanship with something like impudence. In the words of the Official Record:

'The Raid showed that we were capable of moving an heterogenous Naval Force of 252 darkened ships and two mine-sweeping flotillas across some 70 miles of sea through an enemy minefield, and of bringing the craft unobserved to their various objectives on time—with two exceptions. . . .'

It seems that no man could have expected more; few could have expected so much. Yet on the precise and perfect performance of this initial feat success or failure must depend. And in addition, this whole force, so lightly defended, remained immune from enemy naval interference of any kind.

There is no doubt whatever that the vital importance of the timings was fully appreciated, for in the event of any Group (or infantry landing ship) being fifteen minutes late, the wireless silence must be broken. This suggests possible action.

The Plan, in its conception of the absolute necessity of achieving Tactical Surprise, is rigid in the extreme. Virtually there is no latitude. Eight considerable forces have to be landed on eight beaches ten miles apart in almost total darkness, and within fifteen minutes of the exact timings. There is no time 'cushion' anywhere.

Soon after three o'clock in the morning the five main Groups are on their ways to the beaches. The die is cast. At about ten minutes to four o'clock the gunfire of the naval action involving No 5 Group on the extreme left flank is observed from the Headquarters ship, H.M.S. *Calpe*. It does not cause alarm. There is no message. It is imagined by the Naval Force Commander— quite properly—that the destroyers *Brocklesby* and *Slazak* are able to help, if help is needed. The major role of these two ships is to protect Group 5.

The fact that *Slazak* is a Polish destroyer under Polish command, and unused to our naval ways, possibly accounts in some measure for an undoubted error of judgment. One feels that the disaster to Group 5 might have been avoided. In any case, nothing is done; nothing can be done; nothing is known to the Force Commanders.

The Naval and Military Force Commanders are literally in the dark, and this is the unenviable position of the Military Force Commander in particular throughout the whole operation. Indeed, he is forced into the role of a spectator with a seat from which he may only get fleeting glimpses of a shrouded stage, the players and the play. He catches snatches of dialogue. He does not know what is going on.

The following is a passage from the report of the Naval Force Commander:[1]

> 'My general impression during this phase (the period up to and following the Royal Marine Commando landing) of the Operation from a Naval viewpoint was a feeling of inability to give the troops effective support. The Military situation was completely obscure, and the large quantities of smoke drifting inshore made it impossible to see what was happening. On the other hand, had it not been for the smoke, it would have been impossible for the destroyers and landing craft to remain as close inshore as they did.'

The Naval Force Commander further reports: 'Immediately after the landings the landing craft had withdrawn to seaward of the destroyers.'

This was in accordance with instructions in the event of the enemy fire being too heavy, and this withdrawal seaward gives the first indication to the Naval and Military Force Commanders that all is not well. They are in a guessing game, striving to fit signs and portents together.

But the Plan is without flexibility, and there is little that may be done about it. The Official Report comments that it is impossible to carry out a flexible Plan unless the Commanders have a constant flow of accurate information.

Here at Dieppe there is no flexibility, and no information. In the event the Military Force Commander reinforces weakness, and is unable to exploit what success there is.

Meanwhile the column of assault craft heading for Blue Beach is very late at the outset. It is certain that it will be more than fifteen minutes late even when it leaves the main convoy. It proceeds. It is held in a searchlight beam for the last hour of the passage in.

Bearing in mind the vital importance attached to the capture of the East headland the role of the Royal Regiment cannot easily be omitted. But it is too late. The landing cannot, even by a

[1] B.R. 1877.

miracle, achieve Tactical Surprise. The enemy must be alert and waiting, holding the whole convoy in his gun sights.

The Royal Regiment goes on in and lands. It is destroyed.

The Naval Force Commander states in his report: 'The situation on Blue Beach was always obscure.' And he goes on to give it as his opinion that the failure on this beach was the chief cause of the failure of the Military Plan. The Military Force Commander confirms that opinion. 'The failure (he wrote) of the Royal Regiment on Blue Beach meant that it was never possible to capture the East headland.'

What is not clear is whether the Military Force Commander knew, either at the outset, or at any time, that the Royal Regiment was so late. There is no record of any message having been sent or received.

And, had the Military Force Commander known, could he have done anything about it? Could he have ordered the Royal Regiment to join the Floating Reserve had he been aware of the facts?

These points are unanswered.

This seems to me one of the possibilities that might not only have averted a considerable disaster on Blue Beach, but also, in giving the Military Force Commander more flexibility it might have enabled him to reinforce Green Beach in time, and to take the West headland. Some considerable success might then have been snatched from failure. Indeed, had the situation been known the whole reserve might well have landed at Green Beach, outflanked the West headland, and even transformed the situation on the Dieppe beaches.

I confess that the landing of the Royal Regiment held in the beam of that searchlight and twenty-five minutes late haunts me. It seems sheer madness. I do not understand it. It has much less reason than the 'The Charge of the Light Brigade.'

Then follows swiftly on the abortive landing of the Fusiliers Mont-Royal, the near tragedy to the Royal Marine Commando, and the worst is soon realized. It has become unmistakable.

Finally the withdrawal is a most heroic triumph, and the Naval Force Commander pays a tribute to some of those who made it possible:

'Throughout the whole operation, Commander McClintock, R.N., was of the greatest service in his capacity of "Boat Pool

Officer". He was ably seconded by Lt.-Commander Dathan, and Lt.-Commander Mullen. The fact that over a thousand troops were evacuated under conditions which can seldom have been equalled must be attributed largely to the work of these officers.'[1]

From beginning to end of the whole operation military communications have been practically non-existent. Rather curiously the Commanders listening-in at No. 11 Group Fighter Command express themselves as being satisfied that they were always in the picture. Certainly communications between the Headquarters ships and the land remained good throughout. The Commanders at home doubtless knew almost as much as anyone afloat. They did not wish, they say, to interfere at any time.

The communications failure seems inexplicable, particularly in the case of Commander Wyburd and Lt.-Colonel Durnford-Slater in the course of their long journey back to the Headquarters ship with the news of the disaster to Group 5. They board several ships on the way. In all cases wireless communication is either out of order or it doesn't exist.

The main cause of the breakdown from shore to ship is that the Naval Beach signal parties, landing with the first waves of the assaults, were swiftly picked off by the snipers. Those who landed were mostly killed. Many others failed to reach the shore.

But above all the inadequacy of the fire-power available is manifest, and this is perhaps the most peculiar feature of a Plan that depends on a near miracle of complex timings, and continues without flexibility.

In the final count the enemy lost at least five hundred men, many of them in the complete disaster to the Hess battery. A number of light A/A, anti-tank and machine-gun posts were destroyed. The tobacco factory and the gas works were demolished, and many other buildings and installations were damaged. In addition we took prisoner twenty-five naval ratings, eight other ranks of the German Army, one officer of the Air Force, and thirty-seven men.

The German artillery, exclusive of anti-tank and anti-aircraft, it is estimated, fired a total of 7,458 shells. But the traffic was not all one way.

[1] Naval Force Commander's Report.

Our own losses have been fully stated, but a Canadian comment may be quoted:

'From a force of fewer than five thousand men engaged for under nine hours the Canadian Army lost more prisoners than in the whole eleven months of the later campaign in N.W. Europe, or the twenty months in Italy.'

CHAPTER TWENTY-FOUR

THE LESSONS LEARNED

I

At the head of the list of the 'Lessons Learned' on the Dieppe Raid is the need for 'overwhelming fire support', including close support, during the initial phases of attack. The official summing-up states:

> 'It is not too much to say that, at present, no standard Naval vessel or craft has the necessary qualities and equipment to provide close inshore support. Without such support any assault on the enemy occupied coast of Europe is more and more likely to fail as the enemy defences are extended and improved.'

It is realized that it is during the initial periods that the troops are least able to support themselves while engaged in such tasks as wire cutting and blasting sea walls. And they have no time to organize.

The idea is put forward of towing out and sinking 'Mobile Forts' with their gun turrets above the water, and also of providing self-propelled artillery for the assault forces. It is clear that the lack of fire-power sticks in the gullets of those whose duty it was to study the Raid.

After commenting that the destroyer fire was not accurate enough nor heavy enough, and could not support the actual assault at close range, and that a preliminary high-level bombing would probably have been worth while, a comparison is made with the normal fire-power of a Brigade attack.

In a Brigade attack on a two thousand yards front there would have been one hundred and forty guns, apart from mortars. There would be one 6-pounder for each one hundred yards of the objective in close support, and one 25-pounder for each twenty yards of the objective as neutralizing fire. Then for the counter-battery work there would be 5.5-inch and 7.2-inch howitzers sufficient to engage each enemy battery covering 'assault beaches: assault area' with thirty rounds every thirty seconds.

And these guns, it is pointed out, would be more accurate than naval guns because they would be firing from fixed positions. This fire is a strict minimum.

The lessons learned, apart from the valuable information gained about landing craft and the landing of heavy equipment, most of which was being tried out for the first time at Dieppe, are mostly obvious, but none the less important. It is convenient to list the major points:

(i) A great deal more attention was paid to the training of Naval and Military assault forces in close co-operation.

(ii) A raid must be planned to be independent of tidal conditions in the greatest possible degree. A Plan based on the assumption that weather conditions are likely to be uniform is very likely to fail, and therefore a plan which can be carried out even when they are indifferent or bad is essential.

This operation was postponed four times. Even on August 19th conditions were not ideal. If the first idea to use Airborne troops had been adhered to, the Raid would not have taken place.

It is further noted that if troops have not to be withdrawn they can be put ashore in much worse weather, with a wind force of five or six and a considerable swell.

(iii) An assault with the intention of remaining ashore should take place in an area capable of being supplied over beaches which face in different directions, or in an area where a Port or a sheltered anchorage is likely to fall into our hands at an early stage.

(iv) The Military axiom that it is unprofitable to reinforce a hold-up is even more strongly applicable in the assault phase of an opposed landing. In assault a hold-up almost invariably means that there is little or no room to manœuvre.

To put in more troops is likely to increase the target without increasing the prospects of success.

(v) The importance of flexibility in the Military Plan, and therefore the widest possible front.

(vi) Tanks should not be landed until anti-tank defences have been destroyed. And in the case of Dieppe too many personnel were carried on the tank landing craft, including Sappers. The main job of tank landing craft must be to land tanks.

(vii) Unless overwhelming close support is available assault should be planned to develop round the flanks of strongly defended localities, and not frontal.

(viii) Beach signal parties must not land until beaches are secured.

And finally there is the question of taking plans and orders on shore. Three detailed copies of the Military Plan were authorized to go ashore in the orders. This should not have been so. No man can hope to read through, or even check through, 199 pages of a Military Plan in the circumstances of a brief raid, successful or otherwise. Nine-tenths of it no longer matters. And what does matter will be much more easily memorized and available from notes.

At Dieppe three copies did go ashore, and an important part of those, in the possession of Brigadier Southam, was captured with the results we know. The other two copies were found by a naval officer. One copy was on the beach at Dieppe, and the other in a derelict landing craft.

But that was the only serious security lapse of the day.

2

Since a raid on this scale was considered essential, and Tactical Surprise was also deemed to give the only possible chance of success, a naval feat of remarkable skill must be called for. The Plan, therefore, it seems to me, must be rigid in the opening phase. The ships leave their South Coast ports at the earliest possible moment under cover of dusk. They go as fast as they possibly can through the minefield and across the Channel to the Start Point of the raid off the French coast. Without pause the infantry landing ships put the assault craft into the water, and disembark the troops into them. The Groups then form up behind the gun boats, and go in. A loss of even a few minutes is dangerous. It is a race against time.

It is doubtful if the troops could have been produced on or off the beaches a minute earlier, and more than fifteen minutes later means disaster.

Yet given the Military thinking at that time it is difficult to see a way round this problem.

But for the further lack of flexibility in the Plan there is little excuse, and for the lack of fire-power there is even less. Surely this first lesson did not need to be learned as late as August 1942? Had it not been learned at Gallipoli, for example, in the First World War, and in a thousand land battles? Was it not known to every Brigadier who had ever commanded an infantry brigade; and if fire-power and close support is necessary in a land battle why not in a land battle launched from the sea, and against an enemy with known heavy artillery support?

It is bad enough in the cause of Tactical Surprise to be deprived of a preliminary bombing or bombardment, but to be left with totally inadequate fire support thereafter seems inexcusable.

It seems to me that one battleship off Dieppe could have turned the tide. Two heavy cruisers might have done so.

Perhaps it would have been foolhardy to risk a battleship or heavy cruisers. Perhaps the vessels were not available. It may be that in the complex priorities of war, of balancing urgent need against urgent need, the Dieppe Raid sailed with all the resources possible at the time. And it had to sail.

Nevertheless I feel that it would be wrong for me not to comment on these things. There is one final thought that has recurred from time to time: did the failure of 'Jubilee' contribute in itself to the success of 'Overlord'? Would success on that day of Dieppe have deprived us of many valuable lessons, and led to failure afterwards? Was, in fact, failure necessary....

These things having been said in all humility, I pay my homage to the brave and to the dead of the Dieppe Raid.

EPILOGUE

IT SHOULD be fitting for a Canadian to have the last word in this book. On the 7th June, 1944, after the Normandy Landings, Lt.-General H. D. G. Crerar, commanding the 1st Canadian Army, made a speech to his officers. I have extracted the following sentences:

"I think it is most important that, at this time, all of you should realize what a vital part the gallant and hazardous operation of the raid in force on Dieppe has played in the conception, planning and execution of the vast 'Overlord' Operation.

"Until the evidence of Dieppe proved otherwise, it had been the opinion in highest Command and Staff circles in this country that an assault against a heavily defended coast could be carried out on the basis of securing Tactical Surprise, and without dependence on overwhelming fire support in the critical phases of closing the beaches and over-running the beach defences.

"If Tactical Surprise was to be the basis of the Plan, the bombardment prior to imminent touch-down obviously required to be ruled out. Dependence on Tactical Surprise also implied an approach under cover of darkness and landing at first light.

". . . From the study of these experiences (at Dieppe) emerged the technique and tactics first demonstrated by the 3rd Canadian Infantry Division in 'Pirate' exercise last October (1943), and this technique and these tactics were those adopted for the vast combined operation which took place yesterday.

". . . Although at the time the heavy cost to Canada, and the non-success of the Dieppe operation, seemed hard to bear, I believe that when this war is examined in proper perspective, it will be seen that the sobering influence of that operation in existing Allied strategical conceptions, with the enforced realization by the Allied Governments of the lengthy and tremendous preparations necessary before invasion could be attempted, was a Canadian contribution of the greatest significance to final victory."

Freston, Suffolk.
18th January, 1955.

APPENDIX 1

We are about to undertake an unusually complex and hazardous operation, the success of which from now onwards is likely
to depend far more on the actions of individual Commanding
Officers than on anything I shall be able to do from the Command
Ship.

It is partly for this reason that the Operation Orders have been
prepared in such detail, since decentralization in carrying out an
operation of this nature is only possible if all units know previously
what is expected of them and of their consorts.

I hope that by this time all Commanding Officers will have had
an opportunity of studying the orders, and of memorizing those
parts which particularly affect their own ships. It is also essential
that all Seconds-in-Command should be familiar with them.

No doubt, however, unforeseen situations will arise, and when
dealing with them C.O.'s should be guided before all else by the
following broad and simple objects:

  (i) *During the Passage:*
        L.S.I. and Landing Craft: To get the troops there at
                                       the right time and place.
        Other vessels: To protect the L.S.I. and
                                       Landing Craft.
  (ii) *During the Assault and Occupation:*
        To preserve their craft in safety ready for the with-
        drawal.
  (iii) *During the Withdrawal and Return:*
        Landing Craft: To get troops safely back
                                     to England.
        Other vessels: To cover the withdrawal,
                                      and afterwards protect and
                                      assist Landing Craft.

The expedition will be abandoned if one or more of the following losses are incurred on the way to the coast of France:

   (i) H.M.S. *Princess Beatrix* and H.M.S. *Invicta*.
  (ii) H.M.S. *Glengyle* and any other L.S.I. with the exception
      of the *Duke of Wellington*.
 (iii) H.M.S. *Prince Charles* and H.M.S. *Leopold*.
 (iv) H.M.S. *Princess Astrid*.

APPENDIX 2

R.A.F.

TASKS:

i. To provide cover throughout.

To attack enemy coast defences and batteries, of which there are five, including one inland on high ground by River D'Arques, the fourth inland S.W. Dieppe, named: Goebbels, Rommel, Hitler, Goering, Hess.

To attack the two fortified headlands and lay smoke to mask defences of East headland during assault and withdrawal.

    East headland: Bismarck
    West headland: Hindenburg.

ii. Tactical Reconnaissance units to keep close watch on enemy movements to detect reinforcements of garrison by land.

iii. Coastal Command to fly patrols of 'Anti-Surface-Vessel' aircraft in Channel during hours of darkness immediately preceding operation.

Battle directed by Air Marshal Leigh-Mallory from H.Q. No. 11 Group.

Air Commodore Cole, C.O.'s Representative afloat.

AIR SUPPORT:

    42 squadrons of Spitfire   Mark V.
    2 squadrons of Spitfire   Mark VI.
    4 squadrons of Spitfire   Mark IX.
    6 squadrons of Hurricane.
    2 squadrons of Typhoon.
    4 squadrons of Mustang (Army Co-op Tac R).
    2 squadrons of Hurricane (Fighter-bombers).
    3 squadrons of Bostons.
    2 squadrons of Blenheims.

APPENDIX 3

(Order of Battle and principal objectives)

LEFT FLANK

    Berneval—Yellow 1.
    Belleville-sur-Mer—Yellow 2.

No. 3 Commando.
Lt.-Colonel D. F. Durnford-Slater.

Destroy GOEBBELS battery near Berneval.

INNER LEFT
Puys—Blue.

Royal Regiment of Canada.
Lt.-Colonel D. E. Catto.

Destroy heavy battery ROMMEL and attack East headland
BISMARCK above Dieppe.

CENTRE LEFT
Dieppe—East—Red.

Essex Scottish Regiment.
Lt.-Colonel F. K. Jasperson.

CENTRE RIGHT
Dieppe—West—White.

Royal Hamilton Light Infantry.
Lt.-Col. R. R. Labatt.

In support Dieppe beaches:
14th Canadian Army Tank Battalion (Calgary Regiment).
Lt.-Colonel J. G. Andrews.

In reserve:
Fusiliers Mont-Royal.
Lt.-Colonel D. Ménard.

In reserve for a special duty, barge cutting-out with Chasseurs:
Royal Marine 'A' Commando.
Lt.-Colonel J. P. Phillips.

To assist in capture of two headlands, to capture the Town
and hold the harbour to enable the naval cutting-out
party on board H.M.S. *Locust*, accompanied by Chasseurs,
to remove barges and other craft.

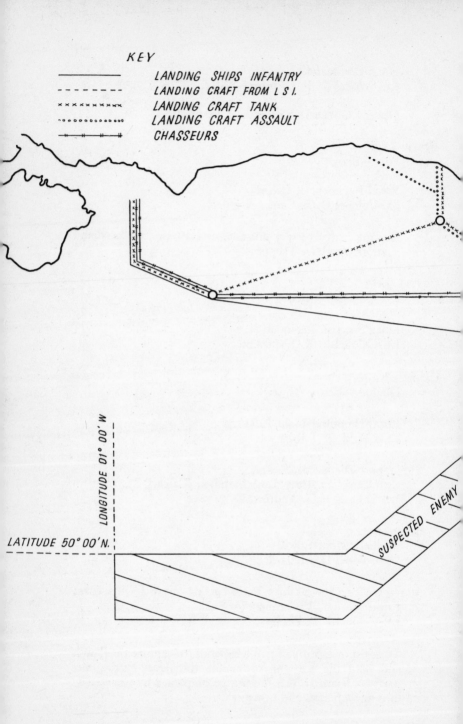

KEY

—————————— LANDING SHIPS INFANTRY
-- -- -- -- LANDING CRAFT FROM L S I.
××××××××× LANDING CRAFT TANK
∘∘∘∘∘∘∘∘∘ LANDING CRAFT ASSAULT
—∥—∥—∥—∥— CHASSEURS

LONGITUDE 01° 00' W.

LATITUDE 50° 00' N.

SUSPECTED ENEMY

OPERATION "JUBILEE"

DIAGRAM TO ILLUSTRATE TRACKS OF UNITS ON PASSAGE, DRAWN ON A TRACING OF ADMIRALTY CHART Nº 2675º

NFANTRY LANDING SHIPS
OWER LANDING CRAFT
 THESE POSITIONS

YELLOW BEACHES

BLUE BEACH

RED & WHITE BEACHES

"JUBILEE"

ORANGE BEACHES

GREEN BEACH

Landings to be covered by smoke-screens laid by air and naval craft, or both, and covered by bombardment from air and sea.

INNER RIGHT
Pourville—Green.

South Saskatchewan Regiment.
Lt.-Colonel C. C. I. Merritt.

Queen's Own Cameron Highlanders of Canada.
Lt.-Colonel A. C. Gostling.

To capture fortified position known as *Les Quatre Vents Farm* and take in rear the West headland HINDENBURG overlooking Dieppe.

Troops will move through valley of *River Scie* to capture aerodrome *St. Aubin* and the H.Q. of the German Division at *Arques la Bataille*.

RIGHT FLANK
Vasterival.
Varengeville-sur-Mer—Orange 1.

No. 4 Commando.
Major D. Mills-Roberts.

The frontal attack on the HESS battery.

Beach ¼ mile E. of River Saane.
(Quiberville)   —Orange 2.

No. 4 Commando.
Lt.-Colonel The Lord Lovat.

The attack from the rear on the HESS battery.

To destroy HESS battery near Varengeville.

APPENDIX 4

OUR LOSSES

Naval:

	Officers	O.R.'s
Killed	11	42
Missing	22	200
P.O.W.	17	30
Wounded	31	167
Died of Wounds	—	8
H.M.S. *Berkeley*		
Missing, presumed killed	—	14
Wounded	—	8
Total:	**81**	**469**

Military Commandos:
(Note: No. 3 Commando virtually not engaged.)

	Officers	O.R.'s
Killed	2	14
Wounded	6	37
Missing	16	172
Total:	**24**	**223**

U.S. Rangers:
(Note: The bulk of the 50 U.S. Rangers were with No. 3 Commando, and did not land.)

	Officers	O.R.'s
Killed	1	—
Wounded	—	6
Missing	2	5
Total:	**3**	**11**

G.H.Q. Liaison Regiment:

	Officers	O.R.'s
Missing	1	3

Combined Operations H.Q. Staff:		Officers	O.R.'s
Killed		1	—
Missing		1	—
Died of Wounds		1	—
Wounded		2	—
	Total:	5	—

Canadian Forces:			
Killed		20	104
Wounded		39	553
Died of Wounds		1	19
Missing (mostly killed)		36	764
P.O.W. Dead		1	9
P.O.W.		119	1,709
	Total:	216	3,158

R.A.F.:			
Killed		4	—
Missing (including believed killed)		108	—
Wounded		40	—
Died of Wounds		1	—
	Total:	153	—

Air-Sea Rescue:			
Killed and Died of Wounds		10	5
Wounded		—	8
Missing		—	3
Missing, possibly P.O.W.		1	10
	Total:	11	26

	Total Losses:	494	3,890

APPENDIX 5

MATERIAL LOSSES

Naval:

    H.M.S. *Berkeley*, Hunt Class Destroyer
    17 L.C.A.
     8 L.C.P. (L)
     5 L.C.T. (2)
     1 L.C.M. (1)
     1 L.C.S. (M)
     1 L.C.F.
    ––
    34 ships
    ––

Military:

    28 Churchill Infantry Tanks
     7 Scout Cars
     2 5-cwt. Cars
     1 Carrier
     3 M/c's Solo

R.A.F.:

    88 Fighters
    10 Army Co-op Tactical Recce Aircraft
     8 Bombers

APPENDIX 6

R.A.F. ORDER OF BATTLE-SECTORS FROM WHICH SQUADRONS FLEW

    KENLEY SECTOR
    NORTHOLT SECTOR
    TANGMERE SECTOR
    DEBDEN SECTOR
    NORTH WEALD SECTOR
    HORNCHURCH SECTOR
    BIGGIN HILL SECTOR

APPENDIX 7

EXTRACT FROM MEDICAL ORDERS

(a) Each L.C.T. of Group 12 will carry two Medical Officers, eleven sick berth attendants and medical stores.

(b) Each remaining L.C.T. will carry four sick berth attendants and medical stores.

(c) Each L.C.F. (L) will carry one Medical Officer, two sick berth attendants and medical stores.

(d) H.M.S. *Locust* will carry one Medical Officer, three sick berth attendants.

(e) In reserve in two destroyers there will be a total of five Medical Officers, twenty sick berth attendants and medical stores.

Senior Medical Officer: Surgeon-Commander W. B. D. Miller, D.S.C., R.N.V.R.

APPENDIX 8

EXTRACTS FROM MILITARY PLAN

INTENTION:

The 2nd Canadian Division will:

(a) Seize 'Jubilee' and vicinity.

(b) Occupy the area until demolition and exploitation tasks are completed.

(c) Re-embark and return to England.

CHAIN OF COMMAND

In the event of the Military Force Commander becoming a casualty or of the severance of all communications with him, the seniority of chain of command will be as follows:

(a) Brigadier C. C. Mann — B.G.S. 1 Canadian Corps on H.Q. ship 2.

(b) Brigadier W. W. Southam, E.D. — 6 Canadian Inf. Bde.

(c) Brigadier Sherwood Lett, M.C. — 4 Canadian Inf. Bde.

(d) Lt.-Colonel G. P. Henderson — G.S.O. 1. 1 Canadian Army on H.Q. ship 1.

Extract from *para 674*.

(*b*)

(i) Each Brigade H.Q. is authorized to carry ashore two complete copies of the Detailed Military Plan (one in each H.Q. craft).
No other copies of orders will be taken ashore and any information required for the conduct of the Operation will be carried as notes.

All ranks will ensure that no orders, maps, photographs, operational documents or notes fall into enemy hands.

Extract from *para 675*.

(*c*) Conversation with civilians.

Any questions about the establishment of a second front or about action which the French should take should be dealt with on the lines of "You will be told when the time for action arrives. Meanwhile do nothing impetuous that may endanger your life or liberty but wait for the call to action. Take cover now, there is no occasion to join in this battle."

ASSAULT AND OCCUPATION
Wing Landings (Orange and Yellow Beaches).
Para 698.

4 and 3 Commandos will destroy the enemy batteries in the vicinity of Orange and Yellow Beaches, sited to cover the main beaches and the sea approaches. In the event that either Commando is unsuccessful it *must* remain and pin the enemy until ordered to withdraw by the Military Force Commander.

Flank Landings (Green and Blue Beaches).
Para. 699.

South Sask Regt. *must* secure Green Beach with the minimum delay to enable Camerons of C to pass through without opposition. Green Beach station will only close down when it is assured that White and Red Beaches are in our hands and therefore that a route for withdrawal is open to South Sask Regt. and Camerons of C.

Para. 700.

Royal Regt. of C *must* secure the East headland with the minimum delay.

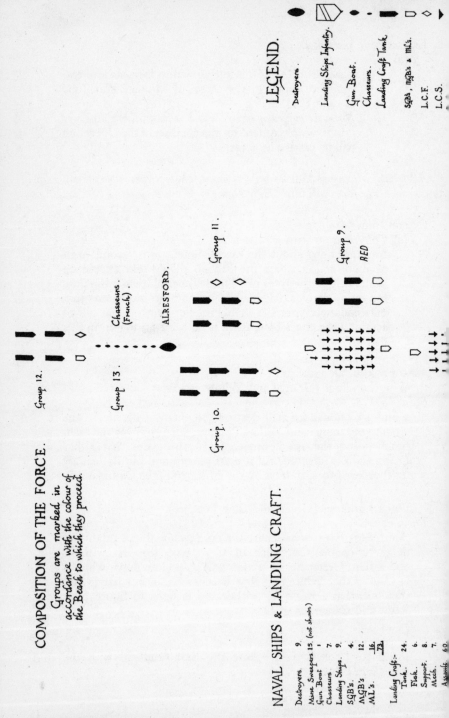

COMPOSITION OF THE FORCE.

Groups are marked in accordance with the colour of the Beach to which they proceed.

Group 12.

Group 13.

Chasseurs. (French).

ALRESFORD.

Group 11.

Group 10.

Group 9.

RED

LEGEND.

Destroyers.

Landing Ships Infantry.

Gun Boat.

Chasseurs.

Landing Craft Tank.

SGB's, mGB's & mL's.

L.C.F.

L.C.S.

NAVAL SHIPS & LANDING CRAFT.

Destroyers.   9.

Mine Sweepers 15 (not shown)

Gun Boat   7.

Chasseurs   9.

Landing Ships.   9.

SGB's   4.

MGB's   12.

ML's   16.
                 ──
                 73.

Landing Craft:-

Tank.   24.

Flak.   6.

Support.   8.

Mech.   7.

Assault   60.

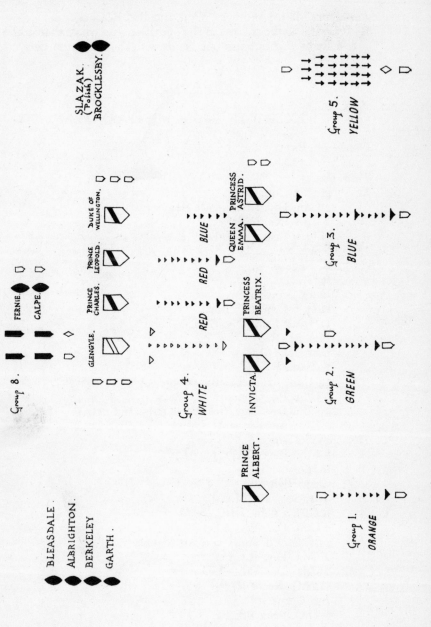

BLEASDALE.
ALBRIGHTON.
BERKELEY.
GARTH.

SLAZAK.
(Polish)
BROCKLESBY.

Group 8.

FERNIE.
CALPE.

GLENGYLE.

PRINCE
CHARLES.

PRINCE
LEOPOLD.

DUKE OF
WELLINGTON.

Group 4.
WHITE

RED   RED   RED   BLUE   BLUE

INVICTA.

PRINCESS
BEATRIX.

QUEEN
EMMA.

PRINCESS
ASTRID.

Group 5.
YELLOW

Group 3.
BLUE

Group 2.
GREEN

PRINCE
ALBERT.

Group 1.
ORANGE

Para. 702. Main Landings (White and Red Beaches).

It is vital to the success of the operation as a whole that White and Red Beaches be in our hands with the minimum delay.

APPENDIX 9

EXTRACTS FROM MILITARY PLAN

ORDER OF BATTLE

Para. 693.

> H.Q. 2 Cdn. Div.
> 2 Cdn. Div. Intelligence Sec.
> 2 Cdn. Div. F.S. Sec.
> H.Q. 4 Cdn. Inf. Bde.
> J Sec. 2 Cdn. Div. Sigs.
> R. Regt. of C.
> R.H.L.I.
> Essex Scottish
> H.Q. 6 Cdn. Inf. Bde.
> L Sec. 2 Cdn. Div. Sigs.
> Fus. M.-R.
> Camerons of C.
> S. Sask. R.
> 14 Cdn. Army Tk. Bn. (Calg. R.)
> 7 Cdn. Fd. Coy. and Att. details
> 2 Cdn. Div. Sigs. (less three coys. and dets.)

Detachments from:

> 8 Cdn. Recce Regt. (14 H.)
> R.H.C.
> Calg. Highrs.
> Tor. Scot. R. (M.G.)
> R.C.A. 2 Cdn. Div.
> 2 Cdn. Div. R.C.A.S.C.
> 11 Cdn. Fd. Amb. and Att. details
> 2 Cdn. Div. R.C.O.C.
> 2 Cdn. Div. Pro. Coy.
> G.H.Q. Recce Regt.
> Int. Corps
> F.O.O. from B.E.F.
> 10 Inter Allied Commando
> U.S. Army

Under Command from landing:
    3 Commando
    4 Commando

(R.M. Commando under Naval control until reverting).

APPENDIX 10

EXTRACTS FROM INTELLIGENCE PLAN

Para. 757. PRISONERS OF WAR
  (b) Labelling Prisoners.
      (i) After searching prisoners for arms, special tags which
          will be in possession of Bn. I.O.'s will be attached to
          prisoners' clothing. These tags will show:
              Unit effecting capture.
              Place and time of capture.
     (ii) Wherever possible, prisoners' hands will be tied to
          prevent destruction of their documents.

  (c) Searching of Prisoners.
      (i) At the Cage all documents will be removed and
          labelled. Documents etc. will then be despatched to
          Force H.Q. ship No. 2 (H.M.S. *Fernie*) by L.O.
     (ii) Prisoners will be left in possession of all badges,
          identity discs, decorations, etc.